Write
BRAIN
Write

Proven Success Tools for Developing the Writer in Every Student

Write BRAIN Write

Proven Success Tools for Developing the Writer in Every Student

Anne Hanson

The Brain Store, Inc.

Write Brain Write

Anne Hanson

 ©2002 The Brain Store, Inc.

Contributing Writers: Karen Markowitz • Michael Dabney • Karen Selsor
Designer: Tracy Linares
Developmental/Managing Editor: Karen Markowitz
Assistant Editor: Gail Olson
Researchers: Stephanie O'Brien • Karen Selsor • Rick Crowley

Printed in the United States of America
Published by The Brain Store, Inc.
San Diego, CA, USA

ISBN #1-890460-11-7

Library of Congress Cataloging-in-Publication Data

Hanson, Anne
Write Brain Write/Anne Hanson
Includes biographical references and index.
ISBN:1-890460-11-7
I. Education—Teaching.   II. Writing instruction.

For additional copies or bulk discounts contact:

The Brain Store, Inc.
4202 Sorrento Valley Blvd., #B • San Diego, CA 92121
Phone (858) 546-7555 • Fax (858) 546-7560 • www.thebrainstore.com

Dedication

To Edie Wagner, my mentor
and friend, who "forced" me to be
the teacher I am today.

*T*able of Contents

You have brains in your head
You have feet in your shoes
You can steer yourself
Any direction you choose

—Dr. Seuss
Oh, the Places You'll Go!

The brain is a wonderful organ...
It starts working the moment you get up
And doesn't stop until you get to the office.

—Robert Frost

*I*ntroduction

While Dr. Seuss may be right about our brain taking us anywhere we want to go, Robert Frost suggests that our brain must be stimulated by our work—our classrooms—if it is to remain a wonderful, working organ. But our classrooms are often far from stimulating. As early as 1983, experts in brain-based learning began to claim that "traditional instruction is at odds with how the brain learns, and the typical classroom environment actually inhibits the brain from learning."[*]

About this same time, media moguls began claiming that American schools were producing students with marginal writing ability. Educators across the country stood up, took notice, and joined in the debate, but language arts teachers were especially concerned. Since this time, we have learned a great deal about the brain and learning, and a well-substantiated teaching approach based on these findings has emerged. Coined "brain-compatible learning," the expression means teaching with the brain's basic operating principles in mind.

With the advent of technology-driven brain-imaging techniques such as PET scans, SPECT scans, and *f*MRIs, scientists are now able to view what is happening inside the brain while subjects perform various functional tasks. These findings, when approached from a multi-disciplinary context, provide valuable clues about the scaffolding that supports the brain and learning. From this, we know that yesterday's classrooms will not work for today's learners. Indeed, "traditional instruction can actually inhibit the brain from learning."[*]

[*]Hart, Leslie. 1991. *Teaching to the Brain.* Association for Supervision and Curriculum Development *UPDATE.* Nov., Vol. 33 (8).

The heart of brain-compatible learning is reflected in the following four core principles:

1. The classroom must be a safe, caring, and trusting environment before learning—beyond that which is necessary for survival—can take place.
2. Each child is unique with a combination of individual learning styles that, when respected and encouraged, can flourish.
3. Interesting, novel, and challenging activities create positive emotional states that increase real learning opportunities.
4. Existing memories, when tapped into and built upon, influence genuine learning and nourish new life-long memories.

These brain-compatible principles, along with many others, have proven to enhance learning across curricula at all levels of instruction—from early childhood to adult education—while crossing geographic and cultural boundaries, as well.

If they don't seem far removed from your own beliefs, great! Educators by nature care about students and learning; thus, much of what we do intuitively is consequently brain-compatible. I hope that, like me, you derive from this a sense of validation that compels you to delve deeper into the research on the brain and learning.* Once we understand *why* our belief systems and practices work, we are well on our way to being authentic brain-compatible teachers.

My hope in writing this book is that educators of all types, but in particular writing and language-arts instructors, will be motivated to examine how brain-compatible learning principles relate to their own teaching practices. I've attempted to spotlight the knowledge that is evolving regarding the brain and learning. I've also provided some proven, practical,

*The *Recommended Resources* page in the appendix will help you locate the research that supports these principles should you become, what Dr. Robert Sylwester has called, a "brain-junkie."

brain-friendly applications that harness the left hemisphere, with its logic and reasoning to the right hemisphere, with its imagination and creativity, while linking the emotional center of the midbrain to the thinking cells of the cortex. These "Real-Life" lesson plans, while tapping into the whole brain, also facilitate the learning of the fundamental writing techniques—description, narration, exposition, and persuasion—and the core genres—fiction/short stories, nonfiction/essays, and prose/poetry.

Ultimately, I want more learners to know the joy of producing structurally sound, syntactically correct sentences that symbolize their full imaginative and logical brainpower. I want them to enjoy the satisfaction of keeping their brains in wonderful working condition, of expressing themselves in the special language that writing is, and ultimately, of having the tools to "steer themselves in any direction they choose."

As good teachers routinely do, you may need to adjust the examples included in *Write Brain Write* to fit the age-appropriate needs of your particular learners. But whether you teach writing to elementary, middle-school, high-school, or college-age students, the Write Brain Write approach works for everyone—even other teachers. Brain-compatible principles know no limits. They are universal! As different as our students are, they are also the same. Tap into the innate power of the brain and you will find the writer in every student. The mind is a wonderful thing to explore... I look forward to celebrating the journey with you.

 Write On...

Anne

1

*B*rain Matters in the Classroom

Serving Our "Customers"—Today's Learners

Yes, today's students are our "customers"—the same satisfied consumers of glitzy video games from which they learn to eviscerate the enemy de jour; the same insatiable consumers of pop-culture music from which they learn to sing lyrics that sound to us "old school-ers" like a crude cacophony. Despite how different our own school backgrounds may have been, we need to view today's consumer-savvy learners not only as students, but also as VIPs—in fact, as our customers.

If treating students like customers turns you off, take heart; there is a silver lining: We don't need to hire an advertising agency or wave a banner on the street corner to sell our product. We are lucky "business owners": Our customers show up day after day without even so much as an invitation. The challenge, therefore, is not how to bring our customers to us but, rather, how to grab their attention and sell them on learning.

> We need to sell learning as a product worth buying.

Because today's learners process sights, sounds, and experiences as no other generation before them has, we are faced with a special challenge. In a sense, we are competing with modern technology for our customers' attention. Even the multiplicity of sights, sounds, tastes, and experiences captured at the mall represent competition for our learners' attention. No wonder so many students equate their classrooms to a sensory desert. This does not mean, however, that we need to be technology wizards or advertising geniuses to reach all of our students. It just means that we need to learn to sell learning as a product worth buying.

As brain-compatible educators, we can throw open the doors of our "businesses" and bring even the mosh-pit bruised and mortal-combat garbed kids into the fold. Today's students represent the largest and most haphazard "soup bowl" educators have ever known. Moreover, many of them suffer hidden traumas—big and small—that influence their ability to behave, learn, and cope.

Seated in today's classrooms are many 6- to 16-year-olds who have learned, out of necessity, to buy and prepare their own meals and wardrobes. Their homework may not seem as important to them as their fear of being alone or their hope of being safe. We know from current brain research that physical or emotional deprivation impacts cognition, often resulting in delayed development or learning impairments—debilitating long-term effects that don't help students succeed in school.

The effects of trauma are as diverse as their causes. We've all seen them many times over. There is the seemingly disinterested student who attends school primarily for the escape it provides, the social interaction, or the diploma. There is the kid who acts out disruptively and regularly enough to warrant disciplinary action time and again. There is the teenager who is teased or taunted while a teacher's acquiescent silence exacerbates the problem. There is the individual who tries once or twice to reach out and, upon failing for any number of reasons, never tries again. There is the learner who doesn't know how to reach out and is labeled a "loner"—with all that the term has tragically come to imply since Littleton, Colorado.

With school violence increasing nationwide, despite more security measures, gun-control laws, and prisons, perhaps we need to address the deeper issue. Can we really justify higher standardized test scores at the expense of our learners' emotional needs? In debating the "back-to-basics" issue, we need to keep in mind that the "Unibomber" was an alleged genius; Dylan Klebold was considered a good student; and Timothy McVeigh could read and write and shoot down an enemy tank with 99 percent accuracy. But where do children learn how to deal with their own hidden traumas—their very real fears, depression, neglect, loneliness, and/or dysfunctional family circumstances?

> As our human knowledge base grows, our responsibility to transmit that knowledge grows, as well.

Teachers today have more responsibility than ever before. As our human knowledge base grows, our responsibility to transmit that knowledge grows, as well. To teach children how to read and write without teaching them how to express themselves appropriately, how to resolve problems, or how to access information is shortsighted and illogical. Our brain (with all its intricacies) cannot be separated from the rest of our body. Brain-compatible learning provides comprehensive, real-life growth opportunities that nourish our hearts and minds.

> "Kids! Who can understand anything they say? Why can't they be like we were, perfect in every way? Oh, what's the matter with kids today?"
>
> —*Bye-Bye, Birdie*

Yes, the world has changed; kids have changed. When we accept this fact, or at least "get over it," we can tackle the more challenging issue: how to help students become proficient learners and writers.

Remembering "Terrific" Teachers

When I dedicated *Write Brain Write* to my mentor Edie Wagner, I debated over my use of the word "force" when I stated, "She forced me to be the teacher I am." Surely it isn't a brain-friendly word. Yet it was the perfect word. Edie forced me to become the master teacher she insisted I be. After much conversation with my mentor-friend, I realized that "force" can be a brain-friendly word. Having established a safe and trusting relationship with me, Edie tapped into my individual strengths that she had taken the time to identify. Each year she provided me with innovative ideas and materials, challenging me to reflect on my fledgling practices, guiding me to create more effective ones. My mentor had, in fact, implemented each of the four brain principles I value. I had no choice! Her care, her attention to me as a learner, her innovative ideas, and the manner in which she shared them inspired me, compelled me, "forced" me to master every challenge she posed.

When I think of terrific and effective writing teachers, I think of my fifth and seventh grade teachers. I learned to write, not from their stodgy grammar drills, but from the visionary way in which they both taught history. We learned about pivotal congressional moments and wars by becoming actors who wrote, rehearsed, and delivered our own lines. I remember dressing up and pretending to be famous people like Alexander Hamilton and ordinary people like a southern slave, both times writing speeches or lines about who I was and what I stood for. I never forgot the fight for independence or the significance of the war that pitted brother against brother, because both teachers made history real, meaningful, and fun—they made it memorable. They intuitively knew that if information was to become part of a learner's long-term memory,

> "When a person manipulates information, or experiments with it, or is asked to solve a problem related to it, the data gets encoded along multiple memory pathways— visual, auditory, kinesthetic—increasing the chance for retrieval."
>
> —*Markowitz/Jensen*
> *The Great Memory Book*

active learning opportunities would have to be encouraged, and the brain, body, and emotions would have to be engaged. Inviting students to become scriptwriters and performers allowed us to learn the new information in novel, personal ways.

It's a brain fact: Discussing, thinking, writing, physically manipulating data, moving, and play-acting are all activities that increase the chances of remembering information as multiple memory pathways are engaged.

Remembering "Terrible" Teachers

To recall a terrible teacher I fortunately have to go all the way back to first grade. She's walking up the aisle. I expect her to compliment the picture I have just finished coloring: Dutch girl, purple pinafore, pink apron set against a field of yellow daffodils, light brown windmill in the background. With her fingernail's harsh tap, tap, tapping, she assaults my paper and my tender mind with an admonishment that I hear as clearly now as I did some 40 years ago: "Who ever heard of using purple with pink?!"

To an innocent 6-year-old, the insult was traumatizing, and the memory has never left me. Had I not had genuinely loving and caring parents and older sisters, the harsh and unkind ridicule of that teacher could have had a debilitating influence on my innocent mind—so eager to learn, so willing to experiment, if only with crayons. I do not remember a single event from my first grade experience other than this terrible moment. And to this day, purple and pink are among my favorite colors. That's how my brain handled the insult.

We shouldn't teach writing if we're not willing to think about *how* we teach it and *how we treat* our learners as we develop and critique their writing. Our methods, especially our methods of criticizing, will determine how students feel about learning, writing, and most importantly, themselves. And, ultimately, they're all interrelated.

Creating Brain-Compatible Classrooms: Four Core Principles

The following four core principles provide the basis for evaluating how brain-friendly a classroom is:

1. Does your classroom reflect a safe, caring, and supportive environment for all students? Before we can learn anything—beyond that which is necessary for survival—we need to feel safe and cared for.

   1. Safe & Caring Environment

2. Do learners in your class feel their unique qualities and learning styles are respected and encouraged? We must feel good about our abilities to flourish.

   2. Unique Qualities Respected

3. In what ways and how often do you facilitate interesting, novel, and challenging activities in your classroom? Positive emotional states increase real learning opportunities.

   3. Novel Activities

4. In what ways and how often do you tap into learners' existing memories when presenting a new topic or engaging the group in a learning activity? When we build upon existing memories, genuine learning and new life-long memories are nourished.

   4. Tap Into Existing Memories

A Window into the Brain

Brain research most assuredly suggests that the human brain is an emotional brain: To the extent that we attend to the brain's emotional needs, we will harness all else, including authentic learning.

The importance of a threat-free classroom can't be overemphasized. But what is threat, exactly, and how does it impact the brain and learning? When students feel threatened by physical or emotional danger, intimidation, embarrassment, fear of rejection or failure, or a perceived lack of choice, anxiety and fear prevail. These emotions, coordinated by the brain's amygdala, can trigger the production of abnormal levels of the stress hormones cortisol and epinephrine—chemicals that put the body in a "fight or flight" survival mode. During this response, learning and other cognitive functions are forced to take a back seat to the brain's priority of coping with danger.

On the other hand, what happens when learners feel safe, supported, and trusted? The brain can relax and learning can soar. Teachers who engage in respectful interactions, communicate in a nonthreatening manner, consistently provide encouragement and feedback, and empower students with a sense of choice create a classroom where learning can't help but happen.

For example, the brain's response to choice usually includes an increased production of serotonin, dopamine, and noradrenaline. These chemicals are known to enhance a sense of well-being and motivation. Choice, therefore, may actually "feed the brain."

In addition, when students are challenged, yet perceive that a solution is possible (and are given the necessary resources to do so), motivation and learning increase significantly. Teachers who refrain from demanding immediate, "on-the-spot" responses to questions, reduce anxiety and allow learners to engage in the kind of critical thinking that eventually leads to more meaningful learning. And finally, feedback that is prompt, supportive, and specific provides learners with a vital barometer by which to measure their strengths, understand and correct their weaknesses, and progress towards mastery.

It's important to note that not all stress is inherently bad. In fact, when we are under-aroused we usually lack the stimulation to perform optimally and boredom sets in. Assignment deadlines, accountability pressures, and delays are just some of the stressors that are part of learners' daily lives, and which, in *moderate* amounts, can help drive learning and achievement.

Meet Katie

For Katie*, her second-grade classroom is the only place she sees an adult whom she knows cares for her—even though it is only for a tiny portion of her day. When she first arrives at school, Katie sits alone, fretting about the night before. *Is Mommy all right? Will he hit Mommy again?* Her teacher, having taken the time to know her students, especially the needy ones like Katie, profoundly understands Katie's seeming lack of attention. Katie is lifted from her sorrow-filled brooding when she hears her teacher ask, "Katie, how would you like to be my helper today?" Katie is rescued from her all too adult concerns. She will interact for the balance of the day with a healthy and caring adult with whom she feels safe. Her teacher, who has taken the time to learn her subject matter well, chooses a book for reading time that will spark Katie's curiosity and ease her distress.

> Teachers who refrain from demanding immediate, "on-the-spot" responses to questions, reduce anxiety and allow learners to engage in the kind of critical thinking that eventually leads to more meaningful learning.

In *Celebration of Neurons*, Dr. Robert Slywester explains that the brain learns best if the environment is safe and caring. How much learning would happen if every learner in every classroom felt safe and cared

*This is not the student's real name.

for? This question focuses our attention on the scars of hidden trauma—a problem that impacts the learning process far more than most of us realize and far more often than it is diagnosed. As teachers, it's crucial that we treat all of our students joyously and with great care, not just our "shining star" students who are so easy to care for, but our challenging "cloudy sky" students, as well—those sometimes misjudged as failures with too many problems, too many needs.

> **"Hey, teachers, leave those kids alone!"**
> —*Pink Floyd*

Caring does not mean babying. Care and discipline are thoroughly compatible! Teachers that discipline fairly, consistently, and dispassionately, groom students who accept consequences and take responsibility for their actions. Discipline can and must be a demonstration of care. Children are wise; they discern fair from unfair quite scrupulously. They need people in their lives who can help them learn how to respect acceptable parameters. They want to be held accountable by adults who mete out consequences for misbehavior or misdeeds without injuring their self-esteem.

No amount of teaching content will help children learn, unless all existing and future educators learn how vital it is to create brain-compatible, safe, nurturing environments where all kids feel wanted—even if only for a short time in their day. Only then will kids see their schools as safe places where they can thrive academically and socially. We can promote a heightened awareness and understanding of the complex learning needs and demands of the learners sitting in our classrooms today. We can do this by taking what we know about how the brain learns best and applying that knowledge immediately to how we teach our valued "customers."

Providing Great "Customer Service"

✏ Let's greet our kids at the door each day, welcoming them to our homes of learning, our stores of knowledge.

✏ Let's take the time in the beginning of each year to set ground rules that support a safe environment with expectations, responsibilities, and rules that have consequences.

✏ Let's make "mutual respect" the heart of each and every rule.

✏ Let's tell learners we plan to obey class rules, too, instilling a sense of trust.

✏ Let's give each day a driving theme of "respect," or "honesty," or "curiosity."

✏ Let's incorporate the suggestions of our learners.

✏ Let's acknowledge that each child holds inside hidden traumas—big and small—that can interfere with learning.

✏ Let's not add to learners' existing scars. We may never learn the size or the source of them, but if we pledge to treat learners with compassion and love always, we may help heal a few.

✏ Let's be teachers who can say that we've never stopped a kid from loving to learn.

✏ Let's be the teachers whose students leave with the belief that learning, while providing the serious foundation for a successful and productive future, is still a lot of fun.

Discovering How Students Learn Best

The human brain learns in a variety of ways. The recognition of this simple truth can mean the difference between a good teacher and a great one. In many traditional classrooms, students are forced to sit for hours and passively receive information. While this one-dimensional method of teaching has its place and will reach some learners, it certainly won't reach all. Rather, optimal learning for *all* students takes place when we acknowledge, respect, support, and *encourage* their preferred learning styles/intelligences.

The term "multiple intelligences" was coined in the 1980s by Howard Gardner, a professor of graduate education at Harvard University. Gardner, while examining the nature of intelligence and alternate ways of thinking about it, discovered that (1) intelligence is largely defined by one's culture, and that (2) the array of human learning styles/intelligences can be broken into the following eight basic categories:

1. **Verbal/Linguistic (V/L)**: Reading, vocabulary, and verbal communication skills, such as story-telling, humor/jokes, and verbal debate, characterize this intelligence.

2. **Visual/Spatial (V/S)**: Students who exhibit this form of intelligence prefer to learn with guided imagery, drawing, painting, mind mapping, pictures, and other visual aids.

3. **Bodily/Kinesthetic (B/K)**: This learning preference is centered in movement and hands-on activities, such as experiments, dance, gestures, role-playing, field trips, games, and sports.

4. **Logical/Mathematical (L/M)**: This intelligence reflects the ability to work with calculations, abstract symbols, number sequences, codes, problem solving, and patterns.

5. **Musical/Rhythmic (M/R)**: Students with this preference enjoy learning through song, rhythmic patterns, music, vocal tones, and environmental sounds.

6. **Interpersonal/Social (I/S)**: Students exhibiting this intelligence can intuit others' feelings and motivations; they are generally very empathetic, collaborative, interactive, and communicative.

7. **Intrapersonal (I)**: This learning style is characterized by a preference for reflection, introspection, strategic thinking, focused concentration, and working independently.

8. **Naturalist (N)**: This learning style is the newest addition to Gardner's model. It represents a particular sensitivity to one's environment or the ability to use the sensory input from nature to survive.

Whatever combination of intelligences or learning styles a student exhibits, we normally have a preference for one or two types and are most receptive to learning in these modes. Teaching to *all* of the intelligences, therefore, ensures that learning happens for every student in the classroom.

When we channel learning through the various learning styles or multiple intelligences, success becomes a reality for every student. This is why the Real-Life Application on page 16 is so valuable. It not only engages students through personal involvement, it helps teachers determine each learner's preferred or dominant learning style(s).

> Optimal learning for all students takes place when we acknowledge, respect, support, and encourage their preferred learning styles/intelligences.

Brain Connection 1-a

Visual Versus Auditory Brain Activation

In what is believed to be the first imaging study that directly compares reading and listening activities in the human brain, Michael and colleagues (2001) report that the brain processes information differently depending on how it's communicated. For example, when subjects listened to a sentence, a different cortical activation pathway was forged than when subjects read the same words printed on paper.

The study suggests stark distinctions in the way the brain organizes visual and auditory stimuli and theorizes that the distinction is due to the fleeting nature of spoken language (ibid). Spoken language is so temporary—each sound hanging in the air for only a fraction of a second. The brain, therefore, must immediately process or store the various parts of a spoken sentence in order to make sense out of it. By contrast, written language provides "external memory" that enables self-pacing and re-reading/review if necessary.

The Michael team found that the total amount of activation was significantly greater in the auditory condition than in the visual condition, particularly in the anterior, inferior portions of Broca's area. Greater activation was also generally present in both the right and left hemispheres during auditory as compared to reading activities. The greater amount of activation in Broca's area suggests that there is more semantic processing and working memory storage in listening comprehension than in reading, Michael reports.

Brain Connection 1-a continued...

Some of the variables that influence the activation patterns seen during reading versus auditory processing are the content of the text, the purpose of comprehending it, and the complexity of the sentence structure. Other research (Laing 2000) points to a direct relationship between reading skills and language-skill proficiency, while research by Adams and colleagues (1999) indicates listening skills are related to vocabulary knowledge and spoken-word comprehension.

 **Classroom Applications**

Realize that the brain processes visual and auditory stimuli differently and ensure that students get ample exposure to both modalities. For example, exercise the right-brain region (activated while reading) through such activities as reading aloud in small groups and silent reading; then exercise the left-brain region (activated while listening) through group discussions, audio-book activities, and student reporting/presentations. During verbal presentations, encourage learners to speak slowly, repeat key points, and field questions from other students. Also have students frequently summarize in their own words what they've heard and understood.

*For full citations, see "References" in Appendix.

Think About It

1. Do you have a disturbing memory of a not so terrific teacher?

2. How did the experience impact you—then and now?

3. Do you have any students like Katie? How do you help them feel safe and cared for in your classroom?

4. Do you make a special effort to stretch beyond teaching primarily from your own learning style bias? How?

 Real-Life Application: *Surveying the Brain—"Getting to Know You"*

In my own classes, I hand out the following survey, "Getting to Know You", early in the term. It gives me a biographical mnemonic or memory tool, for remembering students' names, while also allowing me to set up groups that represent diverse learning styles. The survey is important to my writing environment because it enables me to place within each group at least one student identified as verbal linguistic—who also might have shared: "I'm the one who loves to write!" These students often become my junior facilitators, helping me teach the art of writing while increasing their own pathways of understanding. Completing a brain survey also gives students a strong sense of their own unique characteristics—a great way to start the term.

Getting to Know You

Please complete the following statements.

I'm the learner who..._____

My birth name is..._____

My nickname is..._____

Check only the items you feel describe you most accurately:

_____ I like to draw.
_____ I like to whistle or hum.
_____ I like to solve problems and puzzles.
_____ I love to dance.
_____ I like organizing outdoor activities.
_____ I enjoy thinking about ideas that are on my mind.
_____ I enjoy reading.
_____ I enjoy talking with friends.
_____ I love to hang out with friends.
_____ I like to sing.
_____ I enjoy figuring out codes.
_____ I prefer to work on projects by myself.
_____ I enjoy the game of chess.
_____ I enjoy writing stories and poems.
_____ I enjoy sculpting clay or creating collages.
_____ I love hiking and camping.
_____ I often use hand and body gestures while I speak.
_____ I can listen to music for hours.
_____ I wish I could play a musical instrument/I'm glad I play an instrument.
_____ I like math or anything to do with numbers.
_____ I like to write stories.
_____ I like studying the stars.

____ I like to design new things.

____ I can picture things in my mind easily.

____ I enjoy working on one thing for a long period of time.

____ To relax I would rather go for a walk than sit.

____ I prefer to work in teams or groups.

____ I have a good understanding of myself.

____ I sense when my friends are upset and often know how to help them.

____ I love working and playing with animals.

____ I'm good at oral debates.

____ I like to play sports.

Check only the pictures that represent you most accurately:

1.___   2.___   3.___

4.___   5.___

6.___   7.___   8.___

Add anything else you would like your teacher to know about you:

_____

_____

_____

Thank you!

When students tell me about themselves by completing the first phrase in the survey, "I'm the learner who...," they give me a unique characteristic or experience with which I can connect their name. For example, I'm the one with the broken arm, who plays the violin, has four dogs, etc. Or, I'm the one who stuffed my sister's teddy bear down the toilet when I was 4 years old! I like this visual the best. I use these personal comments or "biographical mnemonics" to learn everyone's names and as a starting point for getting to know each learner better.

The completed survey also provides a valuable snapshot of each student's self-identified learning-style/multiple-intelligence combination, which eventually helps me organize students into learning-compatible groups. By the time I am ready to establish my seating chart—the third day of school—I have already done a lot of work! I've read, analyzed, and ultimately organized students into six or seven groups for the quarter based on their own learning-style snapshot.

Once students have completed the survey, it can be coded with the abbreviations provided in the key on the next page. Each abbreviation stands for one of the original seven (now eight) multiple intelligences introduced by Howard Gardner. Once you've coded the surveys, there are multiple valuable uses for them. For example, you may want to jot down the letter codes (on your seating chart or other daily reference) to remind you of each student's preferred learning style, or you may want to take the exercise further and teach about the concept of multiple-intelligences/learning-style preferences with it.

Key to... Getting to Know You

Codes

V/L = Verbal/Linguistic (purple)
V/S = Visual/Spatial (pink)
B/K = Bodily/Kinesthetic (red)
L/M = Logical/Mathematical (green)
M/R = Musical/Rhythmic (yellow)
I/S = Interpersonal/Social (blue)
I = Intrapersonal/Individual (orange)
N = Naturalist (brown)

Key

1. I like to draw. (V/S)

2. I like to whistle or hum. (M/R)

3. I like to solve problems and puzzles. (L/M)

4. I love to dance. (B/K)

5. I like organizing outdoor activities. (N)

6. I enjoy thinking about ideas. (I)

7. I enjoy reading. (V/L)

8. I enjoy talking with friends. (I/S)

9. I love to hang out with friends. (I/S)

10. I like to sing. (M/R)

11. I enjoy figuring out codes. (L/M)

12. I prefer to work on projects by myself. (I)

13. I enjoy the game of chess. (L/M)

14. I enjoy writing stories and poems. (V/L)

15. I enjoy sculpting clay or creating collages. (V/S)

16. I enjoy hiking and camping. (N)

17. I often use hand and body gestures while I speak. (B/K)

18. I can listen to music for hours. (M/R)

19. I wish I could play a musical instrument/I'm glad I play an instrument. (M/R)

20. I like math or anything to do with numbers. (L/M)

21. I like to write stories. (V/L)

22. I like studying the stars. (N)

23. I like to design new things. (V/S)

24. I can picture things in my mind easily. (V/S)

25. I enjoy working on one project for a long period of time. (I)

26. To relax, I would rather go for a walk than sit. (B/K)

27. I prefer to work in teams or groups. (I/S)

28. I have a good understanding of myself. (I)

29. I sense when my friends are upset and often know how to help them. (I/S)

30. I love working and playing with animals. (N)

31. I'm good at oral debates. (V/L)

32. I like to play sports. (B/K)

Key to pictures:
1. thinker (I)
2. artist (V/S)
3. athlete (B/K)
4. dancing/socializing (I/S)
5. reading (V/L)
6. number equations/mathematics (L/M)
7. music (M/R)
8. nature/outdoors (N)

Color Your Brain: Preferred Learning Styles

◆ Once the surveys have been completed, you can choose to have learners (depending on age appropriateness) code their own surveys, or you can do it for young learners. Either way, to get a preferred learning style "score," count the number of each particular learning-style code and write down the totals.

◆ Now, divide the brain "pie" in the oval provided on the next page according to your totals. If you have the same number for several styles,

these pie sections will be the same size. If you have a learning style that was not marked at all, draw a thick line with the color that corresponds to that intelligence. (You still exhibit this style occasionally, it's just that your brain doesn't prefer it when learning something new.)

◆ If desired, the brain charts can be signed and colored by learners according to the key, and posted on the board next to additional information about learning styles and the multiple-intelligences model. You may want to have learners cut out images from magazines that reflect each of the learning modes/styles.

Brain Pie Chart

Color Key:

Verbal/Linguistic = purple

Visual/Spatial = pink

Bodily/Kinesthetic = red

Logical/Mathematical = green

Musical/Rhythmic = yellow

Interpersonal/Social = blue

Intrapersonal/Individual = orange

Naturalist = brown

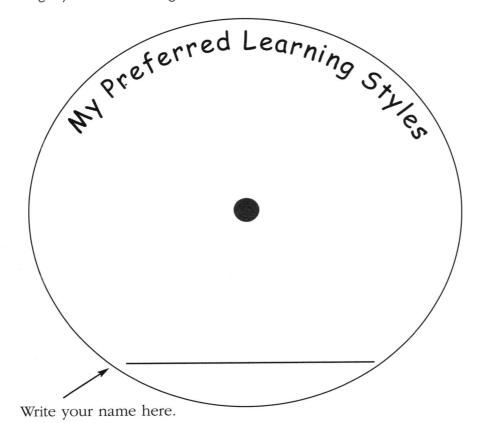

Write your name here.

Divide the brain "pie" above according to the totals from your "Getting to Know You" survey and key. If you have the same score for several learning styles, these pie sections will be the same size. Color the pie pieces according to the color key above. If you have a learning style that was not marked at all, draw a thick line with the corresponding color. (You still exhibit this style occasionally, it's just that your brain doesn't prefer it when learning something new.)

Smart Tip:
Discovering Reusable Magnetized Banners
To free your brain from the procedural trifles of classroom management, try this time saver:

If you have a magnetized board:
◆ Buy a set of magnet clips and brightly colored poster paper.
◆ Cut the paper into strips about 12 to 15 inches long and 4 inches wide. The length will depend on what you write.
◆ Using large block letters and a thick marker, write the words and phrases you routinely write on the board: Copy homework, please read today's goal, etc.
◆ Place these handy banners on the board regularly and refer to them often so that learners come to read them without prompting.

Business card magnets, available practically everywhere, are an inexpensive alternative to clips. Tape the magnetic card to the back of the construction paper banner, leaving the magnet side free to contact the board.

If you don't have a magnetized board:
◆ Punch a hole or two at the top of the construction paper.
◆ Run a sufficient length of fishing line through the hole(s).
◆ Tie a loop in the line and hook it over a nail or tack.

On any given day, banners can provide your students helpful cues as they enter the classroom. Some of the ones I use regularly include, "Please get your writing folder," "Please read today's goal," "Please read the homework board," etc. Letting students know what to expect is important to brain-compatible learning. But our time is too valuable to be spent writing procedural cues on the board day in and day out. Thus, we must get in the play hard, work smart habit. An important aspect of playing hard, working smart is making the work fun. When students are engaged in a well-planned and meaningful unit, learning not only happens, it soars!

 In Review

1. In what way does your teaching approach reflect or refute the four core brain principles presented?

2. How often do you take the time to learn about your students' home life?

3. What measures have you taken that attest to your care and concern for all of your students?

4. In what ways do you provide an enriched and supportive environment for all learners?

5. Do you have some "brain-compatible strategies" of your own to add to the mix? What are they?

2

*T*he "Write" Direction

Writing—A Taste Sense-ation

Writing involves every one of our senses. We touch the pen, pencil, keyboard. We hear and see words scratched onto paper, clicked onto a screen. Sights, sounds, scents, tastes—real and imagined—morph into the writer's words. Direct experience with the writing process teaches us that writing is a very active, erratic, impulsive, and recursive process, and a traditional textbook version of the "five stages"* of the writing process falls short of what we need to know.

*Many textbooks approach the writing process in five stages, which include (1) prewriting/brainstorming, (2) composing rough drafts, (3) revising, (4) editing/proofreading, and (5) publishing/writing final copy.

As brain-compatible writing teachers, we need to delve more deeply into the consciousness of our student-consumers and into the writing process itself. For example, how do we convey on a very deep level that writing, in spite of its demands, is a lot of fun? How do we encourage kids to write, regardless of their skill level or comfort with the language? How do we move them towards mastery, while following whatever mandates we must? How do we balance the needs of students' brains with the needs of the school principal, the PTA, the district, and the state? How can we authentically assess learners in an environment that requires standardized testing? How can we accommodate additional learning goals without additional resources? Join me as we explore a proven approach that not only develops good writers, but also ensures an enjoyable, brain-friendly process that can be implemented by anyone who cares about kids and teaching, despite common institutional constraints.

> Direct experience with the writing process teaches us that writing is a very active, erratic, impulsive, and recursive process, and therefore, a traditional textbook version of the "five stages" of the writing process falls short of what we need to know.

Thinking Outside the Textbook Box

Brain-compatible teaching may not require additional resources, but it does require thinking "outside of the box"—that is, shifting our frame of reference or looking at a common situation in an uncommon way. Brain-compatible teachers, for example, know that textbooks, especially textbooks on writing, will not help students learn to write. They are not real, and the brain craves reality.

Do you think the great masters learned to write from textbook drills numbered one to bazillion? Do you think they memorized the dictionary to enhance their vocabulary? Good writers write...and write...and write. Beyond that, they read... and read...and read...and not just textbooks. As William Faulkner suggests, "If you want to become a good writer, read, read, read. Read everything—trash, classics, good and bad, and see how they do it. Then write. If it is good, you'll find out. If it's not, throw it out the window and start again." Effective writing teachers also read and write and pay attention to circumstances and issues that impact their learners' lives. They reach beyond the standard textbook and keep their minds, hearts, ears, and eyes wide open.

This is not to say that we should not use textbooks. Rather, we should reference them and multiple other reliable resources regularly. The key, however, is to use them strategically without overusing them. We need to know our textbooks from cover to cover, as well as the other books in our classroom, so we can translate the critical information in them to learners in novel and surprising ways. For example, you might give a meaningful homework assignment based on a discussion in class, then have learners self-evaluate their assignment based on a textbook review that coincides with a later class discussion about the questions, concerns, and challenges that arose during the assignment. In other words, rely on textbooks as one of multiple means for transmitting information or tapping into multiple memory pathways.

When it comes to homework, some parents may be buoyed by the presence of a textbook, but textbook drills and readings do little to promote interest in real writing. In fact, when we force students to do things their brains don't enjoy, it's a lose-lose situation. As Robert Sylwester states in *Celebration of Neurons* (1995), "textbooks promote rote responses, copying,

> The best way to compete with the technological wizardry that captivates kids today is to contribute what technology can't—the priceless mentorship that only a caring and devoted teacher can provide.

confusion, and boredom with writing"—not exactly 21st century education goals.

To be fair however, before the technology boom, textbooks played a dominant and critical role in the education process. In fact, many generations of behaviorally dutiful and linguistically oriented learners were schooled quite adequately in text-centered classrooms. But, as Bob Dylan eloquently recognized long before MTV, "...the times they are a changin'." Textbooks today are up against stiff competition. How do we compete with the level of sensory stimulation afforded by modern innovations like virtual reality, interactive software programs, DVD, surround-sound, big-screen TV, extreme sports, and the always-accessible Worldwide Web? The best way to compete with the technological wizardry that captivates kids today is to contribute what technology can't—the priceless mentorship that only a caring and devoted teacher can provide.

If Not Textbooks, What?

Just as professional writers don't always write across genres, neither do they follow a set of prescribed rules at all times or an unwavering schedule. When student writers, however, exhibit normal fluctuations in mood or consistency, they are often perceived as reluctant or weak writers. When our fledgling writers balk at a learning activity or writing process, as they inevitably will, it is essential that we exhibit patience and flexibility. We need to allow them to find their own way, even if it means temporarily relinquishing the "rules" or disregarding the prescribed stages. Think about it: Does a little flexibility encourage your own personal creativity or stifle it?

And, what rests at the heart of good writing if not a pinch of original thinking?

When it comes to creativity, despite complaints to the contrary, I don't believe district-mandated standards or curricula aim to stifle teacher creativity. Curricula objectives are merely maps with highlighted destinations to plan the route. It is still our role to decide if the route will be direct or scenic, nonstop or with detours. Textbooks become the magnified area maps filled with detailed information that we can use to guide students to mastery. We help learners most, however, when we drive their interest in reading, writing, listening, and speaking—not by demanding compulsory assignments from Anytext, U.S.A., but by inviting students to explore the imaginative, magical countryside of writing.

The atmosphere that is most conducive for this journey of learning to write well is one that is free: Free of undue pressure, sustained or high stress, and instead, suffused with a degree of pleasurable intensity. How will you help your learners see that this is a journey worth taking? And in the process, how will you incorporate the critical information provided by textbooks without relying on them too heavily?

Planning Steps:
Brain-Centered Writing Instruction

The following planning steps are meant to serve as a framework only. Feel free to add your own additional strategies/steps to refine your personal planning process.

◆ Study your references (textbooks, ancillary reading materials, curriculum guides, and other available resources).

◆ Prepare an initial "road map" or "mind map" that outlines the highlights of the unit/course you're planning.

- Create a framework that complements the types of writing you will be addressing.

- Decide what order is best to present the subjects/ activities you feel are most important. For example, I always introduce descriptive and narrative writing first, allowing students to begin their initial exploration of writing in a safe, engaging way before leading them to the more complex expository and persuasive writing techniques.

- Refine your curriculum/teaching goals (and those you visualize for learners) in concise and measurable terms.

- Identify useful short stories and student samples that you can incorporate into your lessons.

- Plan vocabulary lessons so that they revolve around terms that crop up in daily readings and around learners' personal experiences (e.g., in context rather than out of context).

- Encourage and assist students (if necessary) to look up unfamiliar terms, as they present themselves in the dictionary.

- Define specialized terminology that will be necessary for full class participation and understanding (e.g., rubrics, criteria, vague, fluency). Introduce such terminology under a variety of circumstances so that multiple memory pathways are engaged.

- If mandated, incorporate the required vocabulary terms. Do not organize a mutiny! Rather, plan activities that use the prescribed vocabulary in meaningful, engaging ways.

- Plan to teach grammar beyond the stated curriculum, but do not ask students to suffer through textbook exercises that don't promote immediate transferable writing skills.

- Identify good samples or models for each writing type you will be introducing (e.g., fictional narrative, persuasive essay, etc.). Incorporate them into learning activities throughout the term.

- Incorporate a range of assessment methods (e.g., self-evaluation, peer feedback, conferencing, rubrics, letter marks, portfolios, etc.) to move learners towards learning goals.

- Create a planning calendar that provides a clear, "big picture" snapshot of the whole term, as well as "close-up" shots of each unit, including daily lessons.

- Locate visually stimulating photos, posters, charts, overheads, and graphics to support each unit of learning. Identify relevant music, manipulatives, field trips, and other sensory tools and strategies to engage multiple learning pathways. Change peripherals often to maintain a novel, engaging brain-friendly environment.

- On the first day of class, and even thereafter, welcome learners at the door with some upbeat music, a few kind words of greeting, and a roomful of interesting visuals. Provide an overview of the term, encourage questions and feedback, and conduct a brief mind-mapping activity that taps into learners' full (logical and creative) brain potential. Focus on free expression and process-oriented learning. Ask volunteers to share their mind maps with the rest of the group.

- When you say goodbye on the first day, tell learners, "Some great surprises are in store for you over the course of the term!" At the very least, this will stimulate their curiosity, and at best, it will pump them full of anticipation.

Building Blocks, Not Stumbling Blocks

As brain-compatible writing coaches, it is essential that we create building blocks, not stumbling blocks to success. When we encourage fun in the classroom, we respond to the brain's essential thirst for novelty and active "hands-on" learning. When we integrate multiple modes of communication (e.g., reading, listening, viewing, speaking, etc.) into our lesson plans, we form the foundation for good writing. When learners know we care, their brain is free to experience the emotional and physical safety required for total engagement. And, when a lesson is so well planned that it engages students' brains in a seemingly effortless way, good behavior, fun, and learning inevitably happen. These are the building blocks to complete learning success.

> "Because neurons thrive only in an environment that stimulates them to receive, store, and transmit information, our challenge as educators is simply to define, create, and maintain an emotionally and intellectually stimulating school environment and curriculum."
>
> —*Robert Sylwester*

At the beginning of each year, I ask my students to write about teachers they've had who were really great and why. Here are the comments shared most often: Really great teachers care, offer choices, share interesting stories, make learning fun.

Time spent discovering who our kids are beneath the surface helps us establish and sustain productive writing classrooms. Whether the rascal, the bright, the sullen, or the one who colors with reckless abandon, we can help them all become better writers. Here are my personal guidelines for bringing out the writer in every student.

First, I believe that every kid is good at some kind of writing, so I never give up on a learner—even the very difficult ones. They all eventually find

> Really great teachers care, offer choices, share interesting stories, make learning fun.

a genre to showcase their voice. My written and verbal congratulatory comments help harness this potential. Once students feel good about their budding abilities, it is easy to build on the success.

Second, I practice patience. If we scold or criticize learners, they naturally abandon their cortex where learning takes place and retreat to their midbrains where the chemical chowder of self-defense abides. Countless times, educators have forced their learners into the fight or flight response, losing them completely to misbehavior or indifference. I let my learners know that writing is revising, is revising, is revising. It takes a lot of patience. I let them know that we writers need to be our own worst critics, and I let them know that we are all in this wonderful, challenging writing game together.

Third, I avoid sarcasm, which robs teachers of the trusting bond learners need to have with their teachers. I do not confuse humor with sarcasm. A thousand times, yes, to humor! But sarcasm is veiled verbal abuse, incorrectly labeled as "just kidding." Sarcasm is not defined as humor in any dictionary. Yes, brain-compatible writing teachers work hard, but working *against* the brain is even harder.

Brain Connection 2-a
Enriched Learning Environments Strengthen
Brain Synapses

Research confirms that enriching, complex environments—
replete with feedback, peer interaction, and meaningful
learning—not only produce better learning, but help the
brain grow new synapses and strengthen existing ones
(Elkind 1999; van Praag, et al. 1999; Woodcock & Richardson
2000).

Animal studies by van Praag and colleagues (among others)
suggest that enriched environments tend to stimulate the
growth of neural connections in the brain's frontal cortex,
hippocampus, and corpus callosum. Cognitive enhancements in
these areas were found to improve learning and problem
solving in normal animals and to reduce cognitive impairment
in brain-damaged animals.

Soffie and colleagues (1999) found that neural growth in
rats continues into old age with proper learning reinforcement. And van Praag found that, in addition to the growth of
synapses, enriched environments actually facilitate the
growth of new brain cells in rats. In early studies with
healthy and learning-disabled humans, some indications of
learning improvement have been noted after exposure to
enriched environments (Grabe 1992; Stone & Christie 1996);
however, more research is needed in this area.

What causes the brain to respond positively to enriched environments? The brain contains millions of nerve cells that produce and send small electrical signals responsible for mental activity. Each neuron connects to another at specialized sites called synapses, where information is transmitted from one neuron to another. Enriched learning environments tend to provide the brain with positive and meaningful reinforcement over an extended period of time, which scientists know strengthens synaptic connections.

 ## Classroom Applications

Enhance learning environments with frequent feedback, challenge, repetition, peer and teacher interaction, movement, music, color, and stimulating learning materials. Augment classroom learning with frequent field trips, guest speakers, outdoor learning, real-life applications, and experimentation with newly learned material. For example, have junior-high and high-school students use their writing skills to rebut a controversial point of view in a "Letter to the Editor," represent themselves in a employment cover letter, or create a valentine's day poem for a sweetheart.

*For full citations, see "References" in Appendix.

Building Blocks for Brain-Compatible Classrooms

Plan to Plan

It's been said that humans invented computers because we needed more space for data, that our skulls just couldn't grow any bigger to accommodate a larger brain or we'd tip over! While oversized brains pose a humorous image, the logic is sound. If we want to be great teachers, we need to record what works, what doesn't, talk to ourselves on paper, brainstorm, mind map, generate new ideas. Our brain is rich with experience. By writing about our teaching practices, we dialogue with our brain! Neural pathways fire away, connecting ideas about failed plans and winning plans, producing better, improved plans that help us to become not just good writing instructors, but really great writing coaches.

To transform ourselves into "really great" writing coaches, it's helpful to rethink how we use our plan books. I use my mine like a journal. In it I jot down observations about what worked and what didn't. Doing so improves my creativity, day-to-day effectiveness, and long-term planning. For example, the following is an excerpt from one of my prior year planning books:

Ugh, you didn't give them enough time! They all wanted to share. Kids misbehaved. Next year, give more time! How do I give more time? I need to! I know some kids missed the point. If I just let everyone share, those that have done so will stop listening. Maybe get kids to share in small groups and then choose a few volunteers to read aloud, while others go to the board and write their best sentences.

The single descriptive word "Ugh" at the start of the entry sparked an entire episodic memory of my failed lesson. The assignment had been to write a descriptive phrase or poem about the bully and his "lieutenants"—characters from a short story we read in class. My intent was to assess what students knew about descriptive writing before starting the unit. After reading the previous year's entry about the activity, I clearly recalled the frustration, and the silly lines, connected to it. My intended focus, which had been "word choice," was lost in the kids' exuberant laughter. Some of the lines had, indeed, been pretty funny. One I remembered explicitly: Red, red, you kicked me in the head; your butt's so big, it's full of lead. Had I not used my plan book, I'm certain I would not have remembered such a detailed account of this learning event. And the consequence of not remembering is repeated unsuccessful outcomes. My journal, however, provided the information needed to modify the assignment based on last year's experience.

The lesson, now reworked, invites students to identify effective word choices from each piece read aloud. Volunteer secretaries listen attentively and write on the board the descriptive nouns, modifiers, and verbs that make good writing stand out. Then I facilitate a group discussion on the writing rubric trait "word choice" (see Chapter 6).

Thoughtfully planned lessons help learners become better writers. Allegations that planning stifles spontaneity and creativity are preposterous. Can you imagine Microsoft or General Electric allowing employees to do whatever they want on the job? Of course not! Functional environments—in education or business—tend to maintain very clear job descriptions and guidelines with enough flexibility to accommodate individual expression and personal choice. This balance is the hallmark that unites authentically successful companies *and* classrooms. Rather than preventing "teachable moments," sound planning multiplies them!

> "The most mature person in any social setting is the one who is most adaptable to other people's needs. "
>
> —*John Dewey*

There's a great line in the (Cuba Gooding, Jr.) sleeper film *Murder of Crows*: "Writing is hard work." Make no mistake about it. It is! And teaching the art of writing is hard work, as well. Therefore, plan to plan: It makes good brain sense.

Just Say "Yes"

We need to say yes to how kids write: Yes, it's okay to "brainstorm" inside your head rather than on paper. Yes, you can write a poem or draw a picture if you think it will help you. We need to say "yes" out of respect for artistry and the creative process. The more choices and materials we offer rather than force upon our students, the more we respect Core Principle 2, which honors each child's uniqueness.

The extra time we spend preparing grammar lessons that use authentic student writing, for example, is more than compensated for by the depth of genuine student engagement, cooperation, and retention it inspires. Kids love solving problems that they, rather than textbooks, have created. Generate opportunities that allow kids to blaze new neural trails of understanding, as they hardwire old with new writing connections. Responding to what is familiar and personally meaningful creates new learning pathways—naturally.

> The extra time spent preparing grammar lessons that incorporate authentic student writing samples is more than compensated for by the depth of genuine student engagement, cooperation, and retention it inspires.

Clearly, we have an enormous obligation to each of our learners. Writing teachers committed to the health and safety of their students and dedicated to the evolution of their own instructional practices create the perfect environment for authentic learning and a lifelong love of writing.

Not Exactly Musical Chairs: Seating Matters

Kids respond favorably to change. Whether it's a change in environment, routine, learning modality, seating, or equipment, new experiences in a safe environment feed the curious brain. In fact, physical change that coincides with a change in subject or focus has been shown to enhance memory. Making a marked impression on the brain, it provides a sense of closure, as well as renewal.

This is why I ask learners to move to a new seat at the beginning of each quarter, coinciding with a change in writing genre's (e.g., description, narration, exposition, persuasion). I also ask students to help me rearrange classroom furniture to better facilitate specific activities or modes of communication (e.g., reading, viewing, listening, etc.). Seating shifts do, indeed, require a bit of moving. But when I need help, I find that explaining the rationale for the frequent changes elicits plenty of student support and/or other volunteer help.

New experiences in a safe environment feed the curious brain.

The charts on the following pages depict the unit seating shifts I've found to be effective. Notice in each that desk and cabinets are in the back of the room, reducing the distractions of teacher activity (e.g., conferencing with a colleague, visitor, or student; a desk filled with scholarly clutter, etc.). Each layout is designed, however, to be conducive to various daily activities, for example, student interaction, "downtime," or processing time.

Since our mind/body/memory connection is better engaged when information is absorbed through multiple modalities (e.g., spatial, kinesthetic, visual, etc.), I rely on peer interaction, movement, seat changes, and schedule changes to keep the environment fresh and novel.

First-Quarter Seating Arrangement:

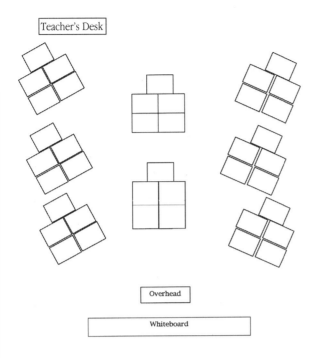

Teacher's Desk

Grouping or "chunking" learners together—five desks to a group—makes it easier to remember student's names and establish learning-compatible teams. When we encourage dialogue between learners, "personal meaning" is enhanced, increasing the potential that the material will be remembered.

Overhead

Whiteboard

Second-Quarter Seating Arrangement:

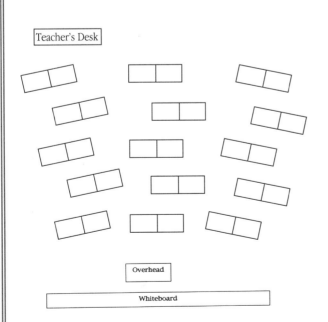

Teacher's Desk

Grouping learners into pairs encourages peer feedback, an important element in facilitating writing improvement. Encourage students to shift from their established seats when desired to form additional partnerships, and to give or get more feedback.

Overhead

Whiteboard

<u>Third-Quarter</u> Seating Arrangement:

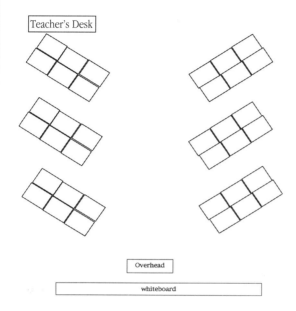

By now, kids know each other and you know them. Larger group activities can give learners a sense of control over their learning. Caution: "Good noise" levels peak at this time, but so does authentic learning. When we allow learners to think, listen, talk, write, move around, analyze, problem-solve, evaluate, and synthesize with others, they naturally tap into multiple learning styles and intelligences.

<u>Fourth-Quarter</u> Seating Arrangement:

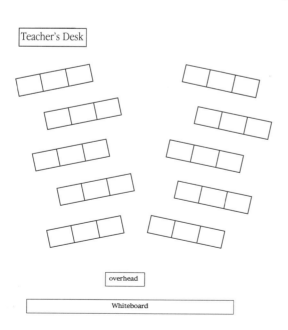

Chunking three students together encourages interpersonal and intrapersonal communication. This seating arrangement is especially conducive to acquisition and application of knowledge. It also supports team learning, such as, investigating topics together, planning approaches and strategies to an assignment, arguing causes, debating, thinking critically, and practicing real-life oral persuasion skills.

Brain Connection 2-b
Bright Light Increases Alertness

Why is bright lighting in the classroom conducive to alertness? Scientists know that darkness triggers the release of melatonin, a sleep-producing hormone excreted by the pineal gland in the brain. Conversely, light, especially bright light, tends to slow or prevent the production of melatonin, thereby keeping us alert and more in sync with our wake cycle.

Research also reveals that even ambient or low intensity light can inhibit the production of melatonin, while sustained exposure to bright light is optimal for enhancing human learning and work performance. Check out the following findings:

* Campbell and Dawson (1990) found in two simulated 8-hour, night time work shifts, that young adults maintained significantly higher levels of alertness and wakefulness when exposed to bright ambient lighting (1,000 lux) rather than dim ambient lighting (10-20 lux).

* Melatonin production can be suppressed by light as low as 2500 lux, Trinder and colleagues (1996) found. (Typical room lighting is around 2,500 lux, compared with typical outdoor lighting averaging about 10,000 lux)

* Although even low levels of light can slow the onset of sleep and drowsiness, Aoki and colleagues (1998) suggest that students should not be exposed to long periods of dim light, such as in a darkened lecture hall.

Brain Connection 2-b continued...

On a related front, Miller and colleagues (1998) found that when sudden and major light shifts occur, two midbrain structures that control aspects of our visual system (associated with circadian rhythm) may actually override normal sleep/wake patterns. In studies with albino rats, Miller found that when the superior collicullus and pretectum—two tightly interconnected structures that control visual attention—were removed, the rodents produced no response to acute light changes. Additional studies may provide better understanding of the role these two brain structures play, especially with regard to light therapy.

 **Classroom Applications**

Maintain a constant, adequate level of bright lighting (at least 2,000 lux) in your classroom. Bright lighting helps reduce drowsiness in class by suppressing the production of melatonin in the brain. Limit student exposure to darkened lecture halls and similar environments for extended periods. When such exposure is necessary, include low-level background lighting (from a hallway or a window). If given the option, utilize natural lighting as opposed to fluorescent lighting. There's some evidence that fluorescent lights raise cortisol levels in the blood, a change likely to impact our central nervous system and cause restlessness, while natural lighting has a calming effect.

*For full citations, see "References" in Appendix.

Creating a "Media Corporation"

Media is everywhere! Kids love it. They succumb to its electric charge of color, speed, sound, and action. The present generation of young learners, without choice, was born into a world defined by high-speed and real-time communication devices and information streams. Consequently, they depend on the intense sensory stimulation derived by such to feed their hungry minds.

> "Memory is not like a video recorder. It's an active, constructive process."
> —*Larry Cahill*

Dr. Robert Sylwester (1995) likens the classroom experience to just one of many channels kids can "turn to." The implication is scary; learners can indeed turn us on or off at will. What is a good writing teacher to do? How do we compete? I say, why not harness the energy generated by the media?

The Real-Life Application that begins on the next page illustrates how we can tap into students' knowledge of and passion for media programming—the Internet, television, radio, newspapers, advertisements, and movies—to engage their writing brains. Whether you call it thematic instruction, real-life learning, or merely a well-planned learning unit, classroom simulations such as "A Media Corporation" provide a competitive alternative to the virtual-reality technology that young brains crave.

As you'll see, each of the "Media Corporation" lesson plans lists primary learning objectives. I invite you to extend or complement these with your own writing curriculum goals. And, although a smattering of reading, grammar, listening, and presentation skills are integrated into each lesson, it is important to add or customize these to fit your particular circumstances.

One way to do this is to incorporate themes relevant to current events. For example, during the year in which numerous tornadoes and Montserrat's volcanic eruption occurred, my students chose to emphasize natural phenomena within the media unit. This focus emerged as a grassroots hook, that stimulated their curiosity and grabbed their attention.

 ## Real-Life Application: *Produce the Image* (description)

In this Real-Life Application, the focus is advertising. An exploration of advertising serves learners across all writing genres and subject areas. The commercial hook connects an existing interest—television in general—with the brain's love of novelty, while tapping into visual, spatial, and verbal-linguistic intelligences. Media is a great conduit for communicating a message, stimulating our senses with textures, visuals, and sound bytes. So, let's.... Produce the Image!

Objectives:

◆ Students will learn how to write effective description, while applying it to other content areas.
◆ The following activities provide opportunities for cross-curricula, interdisciplinary writing practice. They are particularly ideal for helping learners make connections between social studies and language arts.

Materials/Format:

◆ Handouts, teacher's guide, overhead transparencies, clipart, and student samples.
◆ Students to work in pairs or learning-compatible groups before working independently.
◆ Encourage small-group discussion and teacher-group assistance during the learning activities.

Learning Activity:
Writing Sentences Using Pictorial Cues

Instructions:

- Ask students to examine a number of action-oriented pictures or photographs and write a sentence representing each one. You may wish to use Reproducible 2:2 or create your own.
- Have learners share and discuss their work in small learning-compatible groups.
- Encourage groups to identify especially vivid "word-pictures"—phrases or sentences that truly capture the action and mood of the picture.
- Post a list of sensory words on the board as a model.
- Have students compose/revise image-filled sentences, applying insights gained.
- Have learners underline the words in their work that convey a strong image and precise meaning.
- Write several sentences from students' work on the board and discuss their impact.
- Identify words and phrases in the student samples that "produce" the image most effectively.
- Invite students to watch television for "home-work." Direct them to pay careful attention to the commercials, to choose one and write down at least three images that it conveys. The next day, ask for volunteers to share their advertising images, while classmates try to identify the product and selling message. After listening to several student samples, highlight a very visual one by writing the image on the board. Remind students that they will be using advertising strategies to create a variety of images in their next writing piece.

Practicing the Art of Description

Write descriptive words or a sentence to describe a possible scenario represented by each of the following pictures:

1

2

3

4

5

6

7

8

Learning Activity:
Exploring the Power of Words to Produce Images

Instructions:

◆ Have learners share their commercials and image descriptions with each other in small groups, attempting to guess which commercial the writer is describing.

◆ Ask learners to identify the words that "paint the pictures" or "produce" the sounds, sights, smells, etc.

◆ Read the poem "Baseball" (Reproducible 2:3) to learners a couple of times. Then display it over head or provide handouts. Ask students to write down all of the sensory words they can identify in the poem (e.g., squirm, grit-filled teeth, etc.)

◆ Dialogue about how the poem might be adapted for a commercial. What might it sell? (e.g., Baseball is exhilarating; everyone should attend a game.)

Possible Content for a Guided Discussion:
Thin, tanned, bikini-clad girls and muscle-bound guys soar high to spike the volleyball on a sun-filled beach. The purpose? To sell soda. Soda? How does that happen? And why does that work?

Isn't it interesting that the creators of TV commercials rely on the same strategies that we, as writers, do? While writers create images on paper, advertisers create positive (got to have it) and negative (anti-anything) images on the TV screen. Both, however, create images that try to do the same thing: Sell the audience!

Advertisers know only too well how the brain makes meaning from seemingly disparate things. And they know that television is vital in the lives of children. But television commercials can also be a valuable instrument to learning. Every second and every word counts when the challenge is to get a point across as quickly and effectively as possible. Challenge learners to consider the cleverness of commercial writers who bombard the brain's senses with vivid, pleasurable scenes and images—all to sell one message: "Buy Me!"

Baseball

The swift crack of the bat
echoes through the air.

Young men—and not so young men—
burn muscles tearing down baselines
to reach chalk-white squares of safety.

A player slides into third!
Amidst dirt, dust
scraped palms, grit-filled teeth
he triumphs in the shout: "Safe!"

Dugouts pulse with guys who squirm in their seats
kick water coolers
swear and curse at umpires
bellow cheers to their allies
and jeers to their enemy.

Scoreboards flash the numbers
victory
defeat
Excited crowds cheer and jeer.

The swift crack of the bat
echoes through the air.

Anne Hanson

Learning Activity:
Sell Your Audience

Instructions:

◆ Direct students to fill in the circle (Reproducible 2:5) with words and phrases that represent scenes they would film if they were creating a commercial to "sell" or "express" their feelings about the assigned statement: "School Is a Hectic Place." Reproducible 2:7 provides a good working example with a slightly different theme.

◆ Challenge students to be tough on themselves and each other. Encourage them to revise each image until it becomes as clear as a picture. "Pushing and shoving" might become a "denim-jacketed, ninth-grade punk pushing a small boy into a locker." "Being with friends" might become "five girls piling into a brown Accord" and then, "the Accord screeches into the parking lot—five minutes late!"

◆ When each group has at least five strong images, have them share their ideas with the class. Ask learners to listen to each other's images, evaluate their effectiveness, and provide constructive feedback. Are any images still too vague to be staged for a "commercial" audience? Class cooperation will strengthen the weak images.

> Isn't it interesting that the creators of TV commercials rely on the same strategies that we, as writers, do?

◆ Direct the groups to draft a piece of prose or poetry from their images and, ultimately, read them aloud. Again, Reproducible 2:7 provides a solid example of this next step.

◆ Have groups choose an image (commercial) to perform for the rest of the class. The satisfaction derived from group productions gives students the confidence to apply the strategy to their own writing.

Selling with Words

Students' Instructions:

We've been producing lots of images. Television and advertising are really exciting fields to get into. Some of you might even decide to write and produce someday. In the meantime, we all can write about the images and scenes we are imagining right now. All we have to do is realize we have complete control of the "camera" in our mind's eye.

- Imagine you are to produce a commercial selling the idea: "School is a Hectic Place."

- Think about scenes and images using your mind's video camera to produce images of school's hectic side.

- Brainstorm your images in the circle graph provided or in any manner you choose.

- Draft your images into sentences.

- Revise your work to strengthen the images.

- Share your ideas within your small group.

- Sequence at least five of your most effective images to produce a linguistic documentary: "School is a Hectic Place."

- As a group, choose the image you wish to perform. Write the image on the transparency provided (one per group).

- Practice and present your group's chosen image for the rest of the class.

Teacher Tip:
By asking students to watch television commercials with a critical and purposeful eye prior to this activity, you invite them to experience the same rigorous process that advertisers themselves follow to create the image in the first place.

School is a hectic place!

TOPIC

1. When describing how "school is a hectic place," what will you write about? A mood, a feeling, a specific incident?
2. Pretend you are producing a television commercial or documentary.
3. What images will you use to produce your commercial?
4. Which of the five sensory images will you use? Don't use a sensory image that seems false or phony in a quest to use all five senses. Sometimes, less is more.
5. What scenes will you stage to express your ideas?
6. Exhaust the possibilities! Let your mind's eye help you to produce the image! Write words that create the pictures you would film if you were producing a commercial to express your idea.

Student Samples: School Is a Hectic Place

The bumping and hitting of shoulders
As kids run to catch up with friends.
Boys and girls screaming down the hall.
Body odor emitting from packed classrooms.
The bitter taste of overcooked meatloaf
The sour expression on my teacher's face
After catching me cheating.

by Davis, age 13

———◆◆◆———

Short little girls chanting
The mealy taste of eraser
As you bite down with nervousness
High pitched bells and loud kids scream.
Constant chatter behind teachers' backs
The smell of sweat as you rush to class
The scent of perfume on the girl you like.
Sixth graders rush to the cafeteria
As if a fire were chasing them
Heavy back
          packs
            breaking
              spines.

by Jocelyn, age 12

———◆◆◆———

Kids laughing, teachers yelling, lockers slamming
Paper tearing, chalk screeching
The rumbling stampede racing into the crowded cafeteria.
Mouth-watering pizza and its warm, soft dough.
The crumpling of paper when you know the answer's wrong
Squinting eyes, mouth hanging wide open
when the answer won't come.

by Nashelley, age 13

Anger

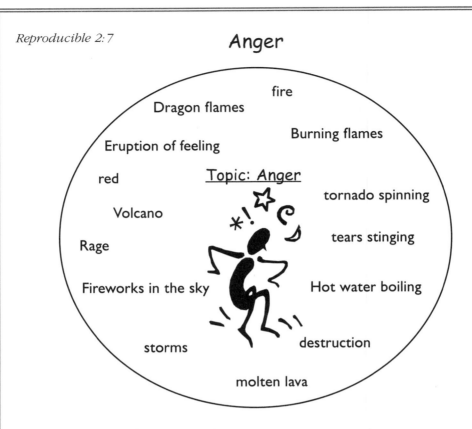

fire

Dragon flames

Burning flames

Eruption of feeling

red

Topic: Anger

tornado spinning

Volcano

tears stinging

Rage

Fireworks in the sky

Hot water boiling

storms

destruction

molten lava

Anger is a pot of scalding hot water, taunting the curiosity of a small innocent child.

Anger is a furious dragon breathing fire down your back. Like a belt of fireworks, it bursts uncontrollably against the smoky, midnight sky.

Tears of frustration escape from the corners of your eyes and spill down your face like red hot lava from an erupting volcano.

Anger violently scoops up anyone or anything in its path and hurls them into a tornado of emotions, then thrusts you onto the ground below.

Anger begins with the dancing flames of a small candle, and builds to a raging inferno.

You sit and wait impatiently for the fire to slowly fade back into the candle and burn out.

You wait for your tears to dry.

Reluctantly, the dragon crawls back into its lair.
The storm has passed.

by Michele, age 13

Integrating Social Studies Content

<u>Instructions to Students:</u>

✏ Apply descriptive writing skills to demonstrate your understanding of specific information gathered within your social studies unit.

✏ Read the samples below, written by students in previous years. Underline at least five strong images depicted in each one. Identify what facts students may have learned within their social studies units on The Columbus Encounter and Arizona's Cultural Diversity.

✏ Think about what facts you've learned from your social-studies unit this year and how you might produce an image related to that learning.

<u>Writers Tip:</u>

The following formula was used to write the poem "the New World". Try it out. Use a familiar place, like the classroom or cafeteria. Then...

Name... A place ⟶ Two Sounds in that place ⟶ Two items in that place ⟶ Two characteristics or smells of that place ⟶ How you feel about the place?

The New World

(From a unit called The Columbus Encounter)

The new world
Its waves crashing, its children chanting
Innocent natives fashion their gold
To hold fragrant flowers that the smell of greed
Will soon destroy.

by Danny, age 13

Note: The samples on this and the next page were written by ninth-graders, except "Immigrant," which was written by a seventh-grader.

Indian Morning
(From a unit on Arizona's Cultural Diversity)

It's the dawn of a new day. The sky speaks of nothing but light shades of red and orange. A warrior is awakened by the sound of an eagle soaring through the crevices. He listens closely as a cascade of water continues to flow towards a small brook.

His people have not yet awakened from their slumber. He must hunt with his hands and his mind as weapons. He begins his quest, sure of his duty and brave in his heart.

He knows that he travels alone, but he is not afraid. Early morning has not yet passed and still he walks alone. Nothing roams the land except for silence and a single saguaro left from a fire started by nature's lightning.

Its beauty overwhelms him as the tall saguaro stands alone. A rabbit passes at his feet, yet is not known to him. He has forgotten his hunt.

by Natalie, age 14

Immigrant
(From a unit on Arizona's Cultural Diversity)

By the dim light of the moon Juan quietly climbs the steep canyon in his socks, fearing snakes, coyotes, or worse. The Border Patrol. Juan is a small boy seeking refuge with his family who's fleeing poverty and sickness.

Juan is not missing his home because he has nothing to look back upon. No friends, no clothes, no shoes, no food, just five brother and sisters to help take care of.

As he changes his baby sister's diaper with one of his few shirts he got for Christmas he feels that he is worth nothing and has nothing he can call his own except the rough skin on his back.

A tear comes to his eyes as Juan stumbles over a cactus. He is starving and half asleep. Juan raises his hopes by thinking of all the nice things he will have when he gets to America. "I might even have my own bed," he softly whispers under his breath.

Skinny, exhausted leathery, sickly, and humble, Juan illegally enters the United States with hopes of a better future for him and his family.

by Desi, age 13

Note: Student samples are reproduced as written—errors and all—except when comprehension would be debatable.

✔ In Review

1. Why are the skills of reading, viewing, listening, and speaking critical to writing instruction? How do you incorporate all of these communication arts into your lesson plans?

2. Of the types of writing you teach, how many of them have you written yourself? How do you think your own writing experience helps or hinders your teaching?

3. Do you use a daily planning book? Why or why not? How do you keep track of your daily successes and setbacks?

4. Is your classroom seating brain friendly? How might you modify seating arrangements to support enhanced learning, communication, and classroom organization?

5. At the end of your next teaching day, ask yourself these questions: What were my goals for today's lesson? Were they accomplished? How do I know? What will I do the same or different next time?

Becoming a Writing Coach

Practicing What We Teach

The brain learns through "rehearsal." Athletic coaches harness this truth while striving to develop the strengths of their players. As writing coaches, we too must train our students for great performances. It's really that simple! Whatever the professional label—language arts teacher, English instructor, elementary school teacher, college professor, or staff developer—good writing teachers find ways to motivate their "team" to practice, to rehearse, to develop their skills, to win.

The best writing teachers also have firsthand experience in their craft. They model good writing. They share their own frustrations and successes along the path to mastery. To sum it up, they practice what they

> "The art of writing is the art of applying the seat of the pants to the seat of the chair."
>
> —*Mary Heaton Vorse*

"teach." To encourage a "yes, I can" attitude about writing, we need to know what it feels like to struggle through the writing process. Not that we all have to be published writers, but practiced writers, nonetheless.

Before I became a teacher in the late eighties, I worked for a publishing company in New York City. As the production manager of several magazines, I learned about editors, graphic artists, sales representatives, and advertisers. I worked alongside these diversely purposed people to produce each magazine. When I became a teacher, I saw that, much like the role I played in publishing, a myriad of diverse objectives would need to be coordinated. I asked myself a question that, with or without corporate experience, we all have to ask: "How do I put this all together?"

In our professional quests to be the best brain-compatible teachers we can be, I advocate the study of various writing instruction techniques. I also encourage continued education in community writing classes, groups, and institutes, especially those that promote a "writer's workshop" approach (such as presented by Nancie Atwell*). But methodology is not the bottom line: We can create a brain-compatible writing environment regardless of our methodology of choice.

Facilitating isn't just walking around, ensuring that everyone is on task. It's being the expert coach who, from personal experience, knows how to groom the team for success.

Play Hard, Work Smart

Planning a winning "training season" for students is not a prescriptive exercise. There are many methods of writing instruction that are effective. The key is to

*Atwell, Nancie. 1998. *In the Middle: New Understandings About Writing, Reading, and Learning.* Boyton/Cook.

establish an overall instructional plan that serves as a foundation for implementing, modifying, and refining daily learning activities.

When students demonstrate a resistance to one kind of writing over another, we need to adjust to their needs. If brain research scientists like Marian Diamond* have taught us anything, it is that no two children learn exactly alike. Thus, we need to have a learning plan—in fact, a multilayered plan—that provides for flexibility and accommodation. If we haven't considered the need for a "Plan B," how might we proceed if "Plan A" fails?

> Clearly we must "hook" learners on the first day the way that good writers hook readers in the first paragraph.

If we all had the luxury of teaching dedicated, serious-minded students, each one of them voluntarily "tuned in" to learning, our jobs would be easy. Their brains would be motivated by the independent choice to diligently apply what we demonstrate. But you know as well as I, many learners only attend school because they have to—because their parents or laws demand it. Clearly then, we must "hook" learners on the first day the way that good writers hook readers in the first paragraph.

The "writer's workshop" format mentioned previously is one of the basic planning tools I use to ensure a solid instructional foundation. Although this format is without question a successful approach to teaching writing, it is not for every teacher. Like any methodology, some of what we know about it may speak to us, while some of it may not. Therefore, though I personally advocate workshop environments, I passionately disapprove when districts mandate use of any particular methodology, as if teaching and learning equates to filling a prescription at the local drug store.

*Marian Diamond. "What Do We Know from Brain Research?" *Educational Leadership.* Vol. 56, #3, November 1998. p.11.

Take portfolio assessment, for example, which was and is still an outstanding teaching tool. When Vermont packaged it as a statewide "pill" and expected teachers to swallow hard, it failed. Enforcing a methodology is an insult to educators, and it does a disservice to the profession. We teachers can be very good at slouching our backs, crossing our arms, and playing the disruptive student refusing to learn. After all, brain-compatible principles apply to educators, too—they're universal, aren't they.

Teachers also need to be nourished by their environments. Each of us is unique with a preferred learning style that, when respected and encouraged, can flourish. That said, the following language arts curriculum represents one example of a general framework from which writing lessons might be customized to meet the demands and parameters of your particular circumstances.

> "Using the various modes of discourse—description, narration, exposition, and persuasion—as the basis of instruction promotes effective writing pedagogy that presents classroom teachers with the logic of the thinking hierarchy."
>
> —*Edith Wagner*

A "Fun"damental Language Arts Curriculum

Each of the four units outlined i the next few pages reflects a core writing skill—description, narration, exposition, and persuasion—and is supported by reading and vocabulary connections. This framework is not, of course, meant to substitute for lesson planning, but to act as a starting point for lesson planning. Since putting the "fun" back into fundamental is basic to the way the brain learns best, think of your curriculum as a pie crust that must be filled with mouthwatering ingredients to make it irresistible. Pile it high with tasty treats and watch learners eat it up!

Fundamental to Language Arts

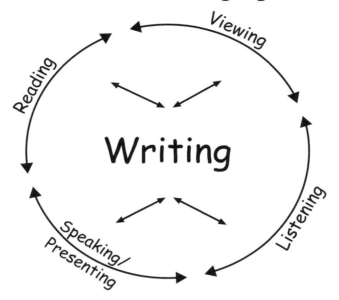

Skills to be developed in a "real-life" context...

<u>Writing:</u>
Types: Description • Narration • Exposition • Persuasion
Stages: Thinking/Brainstorming - Pre-writing/Outlining -
Drafting-Revising - Conferencing - Editing - Presenting

<u>Reading:</u>
Reading - Comprehending - Appreciating - Discussing - Viewing
-Writing

<u>Vocabulary:</u>
Grammar Usage - Spelling - Vocabulary - Writing

<u>Listening and Speaking</u>:
Incorporated throughout all units

<u>Materials Needed:</u>
- ✏ A sturdy portfolio folder w/pockets for each student (stays in the classroom).
- ✏ An additional organizer—of student's choice—for daily planning.
- ✏ A teacher's planning book

Quarter-by-Quarter Game Plan

The following game plan emphasizes a "writer's work-shop" approach, as described earlier in the chapter; however, it can be adapted to any preferred methodology:

First-Quarter Focus: Description/Narration

Writer's Workshop
◆ Description: What do our senses tell us?
◆ First-person (personal-experience) narratives
◆ Peer-conferencing
◆ Rubrics

Reader's Workshop
◆ Choose selections with a specific focus on descriptive prose, poetry, and first-person narratives.

Vocabulary Workshop
◆ Introduce types of sentences: Simple, Compound, Complex, and Compound-Complex.
◆ Introduce parts of speech: Nouns, Verbs, Adjectives, Adverbs, Prepositions, Pronouns, and Conjunctions).
◆ Discuss vocabulary words in context to reading and writing selections.

Second-Quarter Focus: Persuasion

Writer's Workshop
Establish writing connections to
◆ Persuasive communication

Reader's Workshop
◆ Choose selections that generate differing opinions and portray persuasive written and oral arguments.

Vocabulary Workshop
◆ Introduce the different elements of persuasive writing.
◆ Discuss grammar usage in context to reading and writing selections.
◆ Introduce vocabulary words in context to reading and writing selections.

Third-Quarter Focus: Report/Exposition

Writer's Workshop
Establish writing connections to...
◆ Advertising
◆ News Reporting (On-Demand Writing)
◆ Essays

Reader's Workshop
◆ Choose selections relevant to nonfiction writing and reporting.

Vocabulary Workshop
◆ Introduce the terminology associated with advertising and report writing.
◆ Discuss grammar and usage in context to reading and writing selections.
◆ Introduce new vocabulary in context to reading and writing selections.

Fourth-Quarter Focus: Fictional Narration

Writer's Workshop
◆ Introduce the elements of fiction writing: Plot, Setting, Characterization, Rising Action, Resolution, Climax, Plot Conflict, etc.

Reader's Workshop
◆ Choose selections relevant to fiction writing (e.g., novels and short stories) to read in and out of the classroom.

Vocabulary Workshop
◆ Introduce literary terminology (e.g., dialogue, point of view, voice, etc.).
◆ Discuss grammar rules and usage in context to reading and writing selections.
◆ Introduce vocabulary in context to reading and writing selections.

Brain Connection 3-a
Write Worries Away; Improve Memory

Many of us have experienced the psychological benefits of writing down our thoughts and feelings during times of stress—perhaps in the form of an angry letter that we never send or a reflective journal entry about a troubling event. It's likely that most of us have also had difficulty thinking clearly during and after a traumatic event. Now, a possible connection between these two common experiences is emerging—namely that writing about a problem helps rid our mind of upsetting thoughts and thus improves our ability to maintain and process information (Klein & Boals 2001; Pennebaker & Seagal 1999).

In a two-part study, Klein and Boals (2001) examined the effects of expressive writing on the working memory of 71 freshman volunteers. The individuals were divided into two groups, pre-tested for working memory, then scheduled for three 20-minute writing sessions during a subsequent 2-week period. The first group's assignment was to write 'expressively' about their deepest thoughts and emotions relating to the experience of going to college. The second group was simply asked to write about the day's events and how they might have performed better.

Seven weeks later the researchers retested the working memory of both groups. The students in the expressive writing group showed modest improvements in working memory as compared to the group that wrote about how they spent their time. Moreover, when researchers analyzed the students' writing samples for cognitive insight words such as "understand," "cause," and "reason," they found that participants who used these types of words most often also showed the most improvement in working-memory test scores. The researchers conjecture that cognitive insight words help people make

Brain Connection 3-a continued...

sense of the stress and uncertainties in their lives; thereby reducing anxiety about the experiences and freeing up space in working memory (ibid).

Results from a follow-up study by Klein and Boals (2001) revealed that individuals asked to write about a negative experience, versus a positive or neutral one, experienced a decline in intrusive/avoidance thinking related to the event. Further the group asked to write in a narrative versus fragmented format, reported less restriction of activity due to illness, leading the researchers to suggest that writing in the narrative may maximize health benefits. The findings are supported by earlier research that suggests expressive writing benefits people most when emotions and causal analysis are used in their narratives (Pennebaker & Seagal 1999; Smyth, et al. 2001).

 ## Classroom Applications

Creative writing assignments offer a healthy and productive means for improving memory and dealing with trauma. Provide learners with plenty of opportunities to write expressively. Structure assignments in ways that not only promote the use of cognitive insight words, but also encourage an underlying narrative approach and structure. Refrain from grading the content of creative writing assignments; rather encourage peer feedback or self-evaluation rubrics (see Chapter 6 & Appendix).

*For full citations, see "References" in Appendix.

Real-Life Application:
Making the News (exposition & persuasion)

Almost every teacher has been lucky enough, by planning or chance, to experience days where kids seem to be working/playing seriously hard, yet all the while enjoying their work. These occasional moments become everyday experiences when the stage is set for a brain-compatible writing "event." "Making the News" is an example of such an event.

"Making the News" creates an environment kids relate to. The novelty of a classroom turned media corporation keeps them "tuned in." Their brains know this world: It is familiar, yet expansive. The framework is simple: Give the unit a meaningful foundation grounded in clear objectives. Announce the setting. Set the stage. Package and sell the unit to students and parents. Then ride the brainwave together.

Kids, cast as news reporters, advertising managers, anchors, and talk-show hosts play/work hard to produce the reality-based products demanded by their CEO—their teacher! As the CEO, I emphasize the importance of personal involvement in one's own learning process. I act as a "consultant." I talk to students about their likes and dislikes. I help them evaluate their strengths and weaknesses. We learn about teamwork. And we forget we are learning.

The media environment has proven to be fertile ground for growing the writing talents of my middle-school students. Sometimes, I extend the quarter plan into a full semester unit. Although I incorporate all of the following exercises and activities into our "Semester on the Air," any combination of them can be used in part or whole, in a weeklong or semester-long format. It's up to you to customize the unit for your particular circumstances and needs.

Unit Summary

Purpose:
This unit contains learning activities designed to develop skills in expository and persuasive writing. Students explore and identify the elements and requirements of both forms of writing and, in the process, review and apply grammar conventions.

Materials and Resources:
This unit utilizes activity sheets, a teacher's guide, overhead transparencies, and student samples.

Methodology:
◆ Teacher facilitated whole- and small-group instruction.
◆ Homework activities related to classwork.
◆ Students role-play a variety of media "voices" (e.g., news reporters, advertising managers, anchors, talk show hosts).
◆ Students choose the media format they want to use after experimenting with several.
◆ Students practice various writing conventions as they confront "real-life" situations and dilemmas relevant to their "work."

The Plan:
◆ Introduce the unit to parents/guardians with a "Help Wanted Ad" and/or letter home. Have students draft and revise them with your guidance (see Reproducibles 3:2 and 3:3 for examples).
◆ Introduce vocabulary words that are relevant to the various media types (see page 80).
◆ Copy actual news articles, advertisements, recorded news programs, and talk shows to model and discuss relevant examples.
◆ Select pertinent content areas that lend themselves to various media formats.
◆ Make allowances for small- and large-group discussion and teacher/student assistance during each activity.

◆ Small groups can be linked to various media streams, such as a class newspaper, television network, advertising agency, radio show, Website, etc.

Curriculum Objectives

Listening Strategies:
◆ Develop literal, interpretive, responsive, and critical comprehension skills.
◆ Demonstrate how the media informs, entertains, educates, and interprets world events as students identify and analyze the unique characteristics of each medium.

Reading Comprehension:
◆ Develop literal, interpretive, and analytical comprehension skills.
◆ Identify and analyze propaganda, "spin," and editorializing (response to textual analysis).
◆ Introduce language-arts concepts and skills through integrated tasks as students read and respond to fiction and nonfiction and explain and clarify ideas.

Writing Form and Purpose:
◆ Develop expository writing skills. Students learn to communicate (report, explain, and clarify) information effectively.
◆ Introduce standard forms of citing references.
◆ Strengthen persuasive writing skills. Students learn how to present a convincing argument.
◆ Practice strategic-planning skills critical to the writing process. Students learn to organize ideas, prepare drafts, revise, edit, and publish (or present) finished products.
◆ Increase writing fluency as evaluated by writing rubrics (see Chapter 6 & Appendix).

- ◆ Develop grammar, spelling, and punctuation skills. Students learn to identify and use the parts of speech accurately in the writing process (noun/pronoun forms, verb forms, clauses and phrases, capitalization, and punctuation).
- ◆ Practice mixing and using various sentence structures. Students learn to recognize and use simple, compound, complex, and compound-complex sentence structures to convey meaning and engage readers.

Speaking Fluency/Conventions:
- ◆ Develop verbal communication skills. Students learn to use conventional English to express ideas clearly, concisely, and accurately.
- ◆ Develop verbal instructional skills. Students learn to present clear and accurate instructions, explanations, and factual information through oral presentations.
- ◆ Develop verbal persuasion skills. Students practice oral argument and discuss the value and importance of diverse viewpoints.
- ◆ Develop formal and informal interviewing skills.
- ◆ Develop oral summary and paraphrasing skills.

Group Participation:
- ◆ Develop group interaction skills. Students learn to use language concepts and leadership skills to organize and work cooperatively within a group.
- ◆ Develop presentation skills. Students practice oral communication skills within a group context (e.g., oral reports, plays/skits, role-playing, debates, etc.).

Technology/Reference Skills:
- ◆ Develop navigation skills and confidence in using both traditional (library) and electronic (Internet) information resources.

Introducing the Media Unit

The following "Help Wanted" ad designed by my seventh-grade class, complements the permission slip/letter that we send home to parents/guardians as an introduction to the unit (Reproducible 3:3). Other groups have preferred a "press release" format that serves the same purpose. The ads elicit curiosity and student commitment, while encouraging family support and involvement. The teacher-written explanation of the program addresses the most general objectives and reinforces the unit's value to learners. Remember, we've got to "hook em."

Reproducible 3:2

WANTED
Storm Chasers
for Galaxy Globe GBS TV & Galaxy Galactica Advertising, Inc.
Divisions of Galaxy Broadcasting Corporation

Prospective Employees: *Reporters and Advertisers*
Salary: *graduated scale*
Duration of Contract: *9 weeks*
Responsibilities: *Expository (reporting) and Persuasive writing with adverbial, adjectival, and prepositional phrases....plus...*

NEWS

Solid news reporting experience—local and national, fact and tabloid style

INVESTIGATIVE REPORTING

Regarding natural phenomena and disasters

SELL, SELL, SELL

At Galaxy Galactica Inc. you will persuasively sell products and ideas!

Sign me up! _____

Student's Name/Parent's Signature

News for the Home Front!

Dear Parent(s):

Expository (report) writing, with an emphasis on "writing on demand" (writing in response to a specific prompt within a specific time limit) is, for today's learners, a critical skill that is embraced by the most respected names in language arts education. With the reality of state assessment tests upon us, students will certainly benefit from next quarter's emphasis on what is called "demand writing." The natural writing process, which surely is more compatible with how writers really write, provides more time than is allowed on formal state and national assessment tests. It is crucial that students, therefore, learn and practice both types of writing.

I assure you that, while the approaching quarter is challenging, students willingly and enthusiastically meet the "deadlines" demanded by the broadcasting corporation atmosphere. This "real-life" learning unit has proven to be an effective (and enjoyable) way to develop the skills required of "demand writing." Please feel free to visit our newsroom, TV studio, and advertising department, all located within our classroom.

Co-signee required for this adventurous job:

_____

Parent/Guardian's signature

Teacher Tip:
Sending an announcement home (eg. Reproducible 3:2) with a letter, such as this, encourages parental interest in a child's writing development.

Learning Activity:
Headlines and Leads

Objectives:
- Define and discuss the value of a "lead."
- Analyze and discuss the strengths and inaccuracies of the sample headlines in Reproducible 3:4.
- Present the five W's of good reporting (what, when, where, why, and who). Ask learners to examine two (or more) current newspaper stories and identify the five W's in each.
- Assign relevant vocabulary words (Reproducible 3:4) to be completed at home. Present vocabulary in context to roles students will undertake during the unit.
- Discuss grammar conventions in context to lesson.

Critical Definition:
A "lead" is the first paragraph of a news story, which in one or two sentences, answers the five W's.

Learning Activity:
Reporting the News

Instructions:
Write a news report based on the short story "The Man Who Disappeared into Thin Air"* (Reproducible 3:5).

Objectives:
- **Read** and review facts of the story.
- **Examine** theories presented by the author.
- **Create** story notes by identifying the five W's and other pertinent information.
- **Write** a headline, lead, and story (speculate as to what happened).
- **Present** the news article to a group.
- **Evaluate** effectiveness of news stories based on rubric criteria (Chapter 6 & Appendix).

*Short story written by Stephen Mooser, recounts the alleged disappearance of a farmer (Random House Achievement in Literature Series). Any story that lends itself to news reporting will work, however.

Learning Activity:
Writing the News

Objectives:
- ◆ Refer to Reproducible 3:6 and ask students to apply their understanding of the reporting process to the writing of a news article on a topic of their choosing (see student sample 3:5c).
- ◆ Students may opt to write a "script" for a live news report versus a newspaper article. This option helps accommodate various learning styles.

Learning Activity:
Newscasting

Objectives:
- ◆ Using Reproducible 3:7, students apply what they've learned about writing the news to presenting it—newscasting.
- ◆ Students practice relevant grammar conventions.
- ◆ Groups perform news skits, listen to and view each other's skits, and then evaluate them based on rubric criteria for oral presentations (see Appendix).

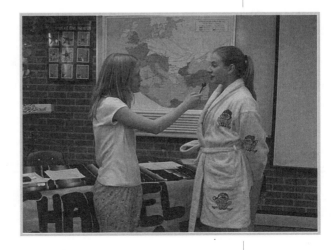

Reproducible 3:4

What's wrong with the following newspaper headlines?

- ✏ Something Went Wrong in Train Derailment, Expert Says
- ✏ Eye Drops Off Shelf
- ✏ Enraged Cow Injured Farmer with Ax
- ✏ Cold Wave Linked to Temperatures
- ✏ Kids Make Nutritious Snacks
- ✏ Local High-School Dropouts Cut in Half
- ✏ If Strike Isn't Settled Quickly, It May Last a While
- ✏ Tornado Rips through Cemetery; Hundreds Dead
- ✏ Include Your Children When Baking Cookies

Write each of the following words in a sentence after verifying its meaning:

- ✏ Headline
- ✏ Lead
- ✏ Byline
- ✏ Newscaster
- ✏ Eyewitness
- ✏ Reporter
- ✏ Bystander
- ✏ Anchor

- ✏ Co-anchor
- ✏ Script
- ✏ Ensemble
- ✏ Broadcast
- ✏ Speculate
- ✏ Theory/theorize
- ✏ Rumor
- ✏ "Spin"

Create a headline and lead for a newspaper article based on a school or family event—fact or fiction—that you would like to remember.

_____

_____

_____

Teacher Tip:
Address vocabulary words as they become relevant. Select a word per day to post on the bulletin board and/or assign for homework study.

Name the Facts: Writing a News Report
Story: "The Man Who Disappeared Into Thin Air",
by Stephen Mooser

Who?   David Lang
What?   Farmer Disappeared
When?   Noon, September 23, 1880
Where?   Gallitin, Tennessee, a farm
Why/How?   Unknown

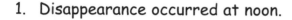

1. Disappearance occurred at noon.

2. Insects shied away from the spot where he disappeared.

3. Judge Peck, Lang's wife, and Lang's brother-in-law witnessed the disappearance.

4. Cows and horses refused to graze near the spot.

5. Wife and two children heard cries for help 7 months later.

6. Both children, 11-year-old Sarah and 8-year-old George, called out when they heard their dad's cries.

7. Geologists found nothing but solid rock when they tested the soil.

8. No trees or rocks blocked the view of Lang as he disappeared.

<u>Possible Headline:</u> Local Farmer Disappears!

Activity based on short story by Stephen Mooser (Random House Achievement in Literature Series) that recounts the alleged disappearance of a farmer.

Reproducible 3:5b

Grammar Activity: Local Farmer Disappears

In the following outline brief, fill in blanks with the correct words:

1. They found that _____ were no holes in the ground.
2. They searched and searched, but David was not_____.
3. Judge Peck _____ up in a buggy.
4. _____ going to discover the truth about his disappearance?
5. There was no trace of David _____ made it strange.
6. _____ not sure what happened.
7. David walked _____ the field.
8. There was a _____ at the farm.
9. The fields were _____ .
10. They heard _____ father speak.

Circle the correct form of the word in the following sentences:

1. He could (of, have) been captured by aliens.

2. Theories had spread (of, about) David Lang's disappearance.

3. David walks through the field as the buggy (rode, rides) up.

4. Mrs. Lang (had gone, had went) to search the ground for clues.

5. Geologists (had come, had came) to search the ground for clues.

6. Witness (to, of) a crime.

7. Theory (about, of) the disappearance.

8. Concerned (about, of) that.

9. Disappearance (on, from) his farm.

10. Confused (of, about) what happened.

Activity based on short story by Stephen Mooser (Random House Achievement in Literature Series) that recounts the alleged disappearance of a farmer.

Adam's First Draft
(As written, including errors)

Man Dissapeares

5 days ago on September 23 a farmer in Galington Tennesse
named David Lang dissapeared while walking in his fields.
Judge Peck Mrs. Lang and her two kid's witnessed this event
also. 2 days after he disseapered Geologist came and dug up
the ground and took dirt samples of the area were he dissapeared. The geoligists said that there was nothing but solid
rock under the area where david Lang disseapered September
26th 3 days after David lang dissapeared A swarm of bees was
around the spot where david Lang Dissapeared but the bee's
wouldn't go around when the exact spot David Lang dissapeared. Could it be a time warp of a murder like some of the
neighbors said. I they don't know, but at this time I authorities they don't think at this time Mrs. Lang and her children
won't wiill find out for a while.

Adam's Revision
(After conferencing)

Man Disappears

Five days ago on September 23rd, Mr. Lang, a farmer in
Gallitin, Tennessee disappeared while walking in the fields.
Some people who saw this were Mr. Lang's friends and family.
When our reporters asked them what happened they all
answered the same way: "He turned around, waved at Judge
Peck, and suddenly disappeared."

Two days after the strange phenomenon, many geologists
showed up at the scene. They dug up the ground to see if Mr.
Lang fell into a hole of quicksand. The geologists found nothing
but solid rock.

What happened to Mr. Lang? Could it be some sort of a time
warp, or an alien abduction like the neighbors think?
Authorities say that it looks like Mrs. Lang and her two little
kids won't find out for a while.

As you can see, Adam's problems were many in his first draft: spelling, capitalization, punctuation, misuse of apostrophes in simple plurals, paragraph indentation inconsistencies, numerical rather than word representation of numbers. In spite of the problems, however, there is evidence of Adam's strengths as a writer in his first draft.

Some teachers might argue that students will never learn the mechanics of writing if they are allowed to be "so careless" with basic conventions of writing during the drafting stage of writing. Fortunately, brain-compatible writing teachers understand the payoff of freeing students during the composing stages of writing. Adam blundered mechanically as he composed, because the safety of a revision and editing process awaited him, where collegial conferencing, both with students and teacher, would filter the strengths and weaknesses of his piece. Hearing the good as well as the bad and the ugly, Adam willingly worked to improve his writing.

Adam's final copy bears witness to the importance of allowing kids to discover their writers' voices. Adam revised and edited his draft until it became the commendable news story reflected in his final revision:

Writing the News

<u>Instructions:</u>

✏ Examine the picture below. What do you think is happening?

✏ Create a news story based upon your interpretation of the picture, tailoring it to a news article format or live TV newscast.

✏ Be as imaginative as you would like, but maintain a clear and factual tone.

✏ Include the following elements in your news story:
- A headline
- A lead (answering who, what, when, where, why/how)
- Supporting details
- A conclusion

Brainstorm your ideas about the picture before drafting the story: <u>When</u> did it happen? • <u>Where</u> did it happen? • <u>Who</u> or <u>what</u> is involved? • <u>What</u> happened? • <u>Why</u> or <u>how</u> did it happen?

Galaxy Globe
Divisions of Galaxy Broadcasting Corporation

Reported by_____

_____

_____

_____

_____

_____

_____

_____

(Use additional paper or back of page if necessary)

Newscasting

Instructions:

✏ Read/discuss the abridged version of "The Open Boat" by Stephen Crane*.

✏ Identify the five W's (Who, What, When, Where, Why) in the story.

Working in small groups, create a news story based on "The Open Boat" that will be "broadcast" live. Roles will include a reporter—live on the scene—one or more eyewitnesses, one or more victims, a director, anchor, and script consultants. Incorporate a minimum of three events from "The Open Boat" into your news report.

After your group has prepared a draft script to submit to your "CEO" (your teacher), we'll have a conference to discuss ideas for refining your script. Once we're happy with the revisions, groups will begin rehearsing their "live" performance for the 10 O'clock News.**

Vocabulary Connection:

In groups, discuss what you believe to be the meaning of the underlined words in the following summary. Then look up the word in the dictionary to confirm its meaning.

*This exercise can be applied to any short story that lends itself to a news format.

**Follow up each "live" performance with a feedback session.

Summary of "The Open Boat"

<u>Instructions:</u>

- ✐ Read the summary of Crane's story carefully. Think about each underlined word and its possible meaning in context to the story.
- ✐ Look up the dictionary definition to confirm the meaning of each word.
- ✐ Write a simple definition of each term in your notebook using your own words.

"The Open Boat" is a story about a <u>catastrophe</u> at sea. A captain and his crew were able to <u>eject</u> themselves from the ship before it went down, surviving by the aid of their lifeboat.

The <u>onslaught</u> of waves from the storm must have been terrible, because as soon as one wave passed, another would come.

The survivors, fortunately, were never <u>disputatious</u>; they were, instead, always cooperative. The captain, therefore, didn't worry about his crew becoming <u>insubordinate</u>. They did everything he asked.

When they spotted land, their hopes <u>flourished</u>. They hoped to <u>outstrip</u> the storm and make it to shore safely. The <u>nub</u> of their problem, however, was the height of the breaking waves. The captain believed it was <u>prudent</u> to hold onto the capsized lifeboat, but the high seas <u>forced</u> them to jump into the ocean and attempt a <u>desperate</u> swim to shore.

Just as a courageous man swam towards the life boat, a huge wave <u>simultaneously</u> lifted the forlorn crew up and into shallow water, <u>quenching</u> everyone's thirst for safety.

Teacher Tip:
Don't ask students to write definitions word-for-word from the dictionary. Such assignments don't represent authentic use of the dictionary, nor are they brain-compatible or writing-friendly.

Creating Complex Sentences—
Vocabulary Grab Bag

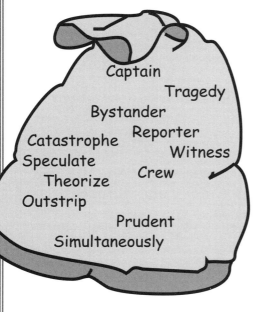

Captain
Tragedy
Bystander
Reporter
Catastrophe
Speculate Witness
Crew
Theorize
Outstrip
Prudent
Simultaneously

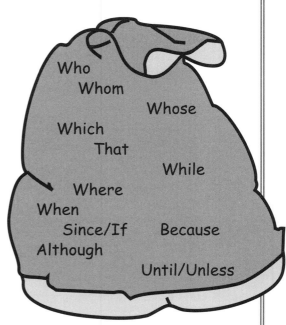

Who
Whom
Whose
Which
That
While
Where
When
Since/If Because
Although
Until/Unless

Instructions:

✏ Choose one word from the left bag and one from the right.

✏ Write a sentence that correctly combines the two words, completing the sentence with additional words of your choice.

✏ Repeat the exercise five times using different words from the grab bags for each sentence. Check off words in the grab bags as you use them and underline them in your sentences.

✏ Combine the five sentences into a cohesive paragraph.

Teacher Tip:
Vocabulary activities such as these are very useful for substitute-teacher days. They're easy to facilitate and can help kids stay on task with the planned curriculum despite your absence.

Learning Activity:

Exploring the World of Advertising

Objectives:

◆ Students will learn about and use advertising techniques to express their opinions.

◆ Students will examine and discuss how point-of-view and habits (e.g., consumer buying) are influenced by persuasive writing.

◆ Discuss how written persuasion techniques relate to debate practice.

Instructions (Part 1):

◆ Distribute pre-prepared packets (1 per group) containing magazine advertisements of a particular product type (e.g., sports equipment, cars, cleaning products, make up, etc.).

◆ Ask groups to examine the contents of their packets and discuss how advertisers persuade consumers to buy a particular product.

You may want to hand out a worksheet, such as Reproducible 3:9 to help guide the group's discussion.

Instructions (Part 2):

◆ Have teams create an ad to sell a product of their choice.

◆ Ask teams to write a slogan or tagline, create vivid and interesting copy, and demonstrate effective layout techniques.

◆ Have teams present their ads to the class, fielding questions and receiving feedback.

◆ Close with a whole-group discussion about the various team members involved in producing an ad. (e.g., photographers, graphic artists, desktop publishers, models, stunt personnel, sales representatives, copy writers, editors, production managers, printers, etc.).

What Is In an Ad?

Look through your packet of ads and respond to the following questions:

- ✏ What is the name of the product being advertised?
- ✏ What kind of product is it?
- ✏ Does the ad feature a slogan, tagline, or catchy phrase?
- ✏ How much copy does the ad contain? What does it convey?
- ✏ What does the primary picture or photograph in the ad depict?
- ✏ How is the picture/photograph or theme of the ad used to sell the product?
- ✏ Why do you think the advertisers chose this image to sell their product?
- ✏ What type of advertising strategy (e.g., bandwagon, testimonial, emotional, etc.) does this ad employ? Note: It may use more than one.

Vocabulary Connection:

- ✏ Bandwagon—Hard sell; everyone else is doing it, so should you!
- ✏ Testimonial—Direct quotes of famous people and satisfied customers.
- ✏ Emotional—Use of a feeling or emotion for appeal; if you buy this product, you'll feel happy.

Teacher Tips:
Asking what they already know is a great way to invite learners into the next activity.

Auditory and visual, as well as spatial and kinesthetic learners benefit from the "good noise" environment—the sounds of learners interacting to accomplish a learning goal—that this activity generates.

Learning Activity:
Putting It All Together

Volcanoes, tornadoes, hurricanes, and earthquakes hold curiosity, excitement, and adventure for students. In 1998, my students showed a particular interest in the tornadoes that unexpectedly ravished parts of Florida. I realized I had

the perfect hook to reel them in for the district-required test on summary (expository) writing: They became "Storm Chasers" exploring "Nature's Fury" (see Reproducible 3:12)

I created a prompt for summary writing (Reproducible 3:10) that incorporated our "Semester on the Air" theme. I told the class that the target audience for their summaries was the producer of our school's TV station. The learning activity met my personal goals to teach the writing skills critical to exposition—organizing information, distinguishing relevant from irrelevant facts and details, summarizing facts, and writing the summary report (Reproducible 3:11). It *also* satisfied the following objectives required by my district's curriculum guide:

Objectives:
◆ To write a summary presenting clearly expressed, organized information in learner's own words, using correct grammar, spelling, and punctuation.
◆ To organize ideas through the use of techniques such as mapping, categorizing, outlining, and note taking.
◆ To narrow a topic from general to more specific.

Your Assignment

Your TV station's producer is deciding whether to produce a show on the fury of tornadoes. She directs you to do some research and write a summary about tornadoes. Based on your findings, she will decide whether or not to produce the show.

What kinds of facts will be important to use in your summary?

<u>Note</u>: Before going to final copy, use the following summary checklist, both alone and with a partner, to make sure you have met all the criteria for a persuasive summary.

<u>Summary Checklist</u>

My statements are...	Yes	Not Yet
Accurate:	☐	☐
Concise:	☐	☐
Essential:	☐	☐
I have included supporting details:	☐	☐
I have used effective and clear language:	☐	☐
Others will get the main idea of the topic by reading my summary:	☐	☐

One Student's Summary:
"A Tornado's Fury"

Tornadoes, most powerful whirling windstorms on earth. Winds in a tornado can reach more than 200 miles per hour. Tornadoes hit the United States more than any other place on earth. Tornadoes in the United States start by cold, dry air and wet, humid air from the Gulf of Mexico meeting. Most of the time these two fronts meet over the Mid-Western states, also known as Tornado Alley, U.S.A. Tornadoes occur spring to early summer on hot, humid days, from afternoon to early

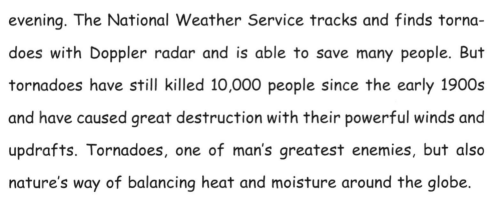

evening. The National Weather Service tracks and finds tornadoes with Doppler radar and is able to save many people. But tornadoes have still killed 10,000 people since the early 1900s and have caused great destruction with their powerful winds and updrafts. Tornadoes, one of man's greatest enemies, but also nature's way of balancing heat and moisture around the globe.

By Katie, age 12

The sample summary (Reproducible 3:11) meets all of the rubric criteria for a well-written summary report. It is accurate and concise. It includes essential and supporting details. It clearly summarizes the fury of tornadoes. The writer hooks the reader with an image of whirling winds, proceeds with "documentary worthy" details, and ends by defining tornadoes as one of man's greatest enemies. The student's organizational decisions provide an inviting start and a satisfying conclusion with interesting, informative facts in between.

After summaries have been completed, I challenge students to write a live-at-the-scene news report about a tornado strike. Working in groups, they must determine roles for the production (e.g., anchor, eyewitnesses, survivors, daredevil storm chasers, news director, etc.) and carry it out.

This activity exercises the thinking, collaborative writing, and presentation skills of the presenting group, while the viewing group practices its listening and viewing skills in an entertaining format.

Learning Activity:
Using Facts to Communicate Opinion

Objectives:

◆ Using a fictitious scenario, students learn the difference between opinion and fact and logical reasoning and emotional appeal.
◆ The prompts and formats used (e.g., talk show, debate, op/ed page) engage learners because the subjects chosen are relevant to their lives. For example, my students created "The Not-So-Rikkie Lake Show"(Reproducible 3:13)—a mock talk show that explored persuasive argument through the star-crossed characters Kim and Joe.

◆ Students learn how to use facts to support opinions. Learning and using the elements of persuasion in an entertaining format prepares students for formal argument assessment later.

Format:

◆ The media connection continues: *The Not-So-Rikkie Lake Show* sets the scene for the debate. Kids plan and present their arguments within the talk show format. (*The Not-So-Jerry Springer Show* works equally well, but chair throwing is definitely prohibited.)

◆ Letters to Kim: Students who do not wish to argue orally write persuasive letters to the show's guest, Kim. They are directed to write to Kim after seeing her on the talk show.

Follow-Up:

If you wish to extend the lesson, you might have students write an opinion essay. One of my language arts curriculum objectives states: "Students will write an opinion essay based on a specific prompt."

Within the media environment, a natural format for an opinion essay is a newspaper editorial. My students, having grown so much since their early reporting and rookie advertising days are promoted to editors and asked to write feature editorials in subsequent quarters.

 Think About It

What issues, topics, and formats will spark your students' interest? Remember... Open <u>your</u> ears and eyes, talk to your learners, and show interest in their concerns, dreams, feelings, and experiences.

Nature's Fury

Instructions:

- ✎ Recall and apply information gathered from articles, videos, and literature involving man-made and natural disasters.
- ✎ Analyze the information, drawing conclusions and forming opinions.
- ✎ Organize the information and write an opinion essay (exposition) in the format of a newspaper editorial.

Your Assignment:

This is it! You've been promoted to editorial writer. The editorial you write will appear on the front page of our class newspaper. Using acquired knowledge about nature—as discovered through our research and readings about volcanoes, tornadoes, and storms—write your editorial by responding to the following question:

Man Versus Nature:
And the winner is...

_____

_____

_____

_____

_____

_____

_____

_____

_____

_____

_____

The Not-So-Rikkie Lake Show

Instructions:

- ✏ Review the facts about the characters in the prompt below and decide how to advise them.
- ✏ In small groups, discuss how to distinguish facts from opinions.

Prompt:

The show's guest, Kim, is upset because she is not sure whether she should break up with Joe, a boy she's been dating for two months. Will you persuade Kim to stay with Joe or to stop seeing him?

Facts:

Joe is 15. Kim is 12.
Joe bought Kim two gold chains and a bracelet.
Joe first asked Kim out on a dare made by his friends.
Joe does not allow Kim to hang out with her friends.
Their two-month anniversary will be next Friday.
Joe left Kim at the dance to be with his friends.

Teacher Tip:
Each fact can be used *for* or *against* Joe. Let learners discuss and debate until they realize that facts must be assigned reasoning to form opinions that can be supported. For example, buying two gold chains and a bracelet is a fact, but does it show Joe's genuine care and generosity. . .or his conniving plans to buy Kim's love?

Brain Connection 3-b
Puzzles Prime the Brain for Problem-Solving

When encountering a mental block, research suggests that taking a brain-break and focusing on a puzzle or word game may help solve the problem. Puzzles, word games, and brain teasers stimulate activity in the brain's frontal lobe and right hemisphere, making neural connections more flexible for future problem-solving, report researchers (Fan & Gruenfeld, 1998; Gebers 1985; Malouff & Schutte 1998).

Stimulating brain activities not only give the brain a break from more serious concerns, but they contribute to the development of thinking skills, creativity, and individual discovery. These benefits are compounded when two or more learners work together on puzzles and brainteasers (Gebers 1985). Brain games not only promote cooperative social interaction, they provide constructive classroom activity while teachers are engaged in one-on-one learning with other students.

 ## Classroom Applications

Consider setting up a brain-break area in the classroom that includes games such as Scrabble, Clue, brainteasers, books/cards, word-search puzzles, crossword puzzles, etc. I have found that such activities are perfect for learners who complete assignments early, have writers' block, or need (and deserve) a break from the regular classroom routine. You can enhance meaning and recall during brain-breaks by incorporating subject content into word games and puzzles. Consider setting up a brain-break area in the classroom that includes games such as Scrabble, Clue, brainteasers, books/cards, word-search puzzles, crossword puzzles, etc.

*For full citations, see "References" in Appendix.

I hope that you will experiment with these "Semester on the Air" activities. If you do, I know that you'll witness groups of learners who willingly immerse themselves in hard work/fun every day. In striving to imitate and apply what they know so well about the media, students will embrace their "job" assignments. Ask them for feedback. You'll see. The most common suggestion I get is, "Can we do more of this? It was fun!"

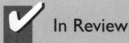 In Review

1. What kinds of writing are you required to teach?

2. What strategies do you use to "hook" learners?

3. What brain principles apply to your approach for engaging learners?

4. How do you integrate reading, grammar, listening, and presentation skills into your writing lessons?

5. In what ways do you create relevant content links to learners' real-life situations and experiences?

Building Bridges Across Neuropathways

The Seven Stages of Brain-Friendly Writing Instruction

With John,* one of my middle-school students, as a case study, let's examine the seven stages of teaching writing with the brain in mind. The following

*This is not the student's real name.

flow chart depicts the symbiotic relationship of the seven stages:

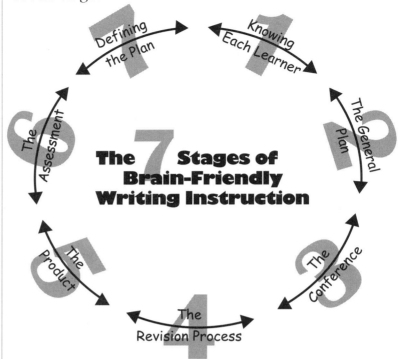

The 7 Stages of Brain-Friendly Writing Instruction

1 Knowing Each Learner
2 The General Plan
3 The Conference
4 The Revision Process
5 The Product
6 The Assessment
7 Defining the Plan

In summary, I first gather clues about John, his learning-style preferences, and his home life (stage 1). Then I mold a general plan with his learning-style preferences in mind (stage 2). Once John completes his first writing exercises, I conference with him, reviewing the strengths and areas for improvement in his writing (stage 3). Once he revises his work (stage 4) and "finalizes" the piece (stage 5), we do a cooperative assessment (stage 6) and refine John's learning plan (stage 7).

Stage 1: Knowing Each Learner

John was a quiet loner. He spoke when called upon, read aloud adequately, but never volunteered. Although he contributed some to group activities with the encouragement of his classmates, he did not converse well. He swallowed hard and often and displayed physical discomfort when spoken to, no matter how gently. In an effort to ease his dis-ease, I used neutral tones and succinct directives when speaking to him.

On the first day of school, John indicated in his "brain survey" (Chapter 1) that he enjoyed music, which would later become the topic of his first writing assignment. He also revealed a vital bit of personal information when he completed the sentence, "I'm the one who... has *seven* sisters." These facets of John's life—his love of music and his "crowded" home environment—later helped me to determine what cues might motivate him to write.

Stage 2: The General Plan

To prepare John and his classmates for the new quarter, I had the class complete three brief writing exercises that focused on using our five senses to evoke powerful images in our writing (Chapter 2). We often tend to reduce the task of descriptive writing to the mundane: "I could smell the sweet candy. I could taste it, too." To maximize learner success, I challenged them to imagine a camera in their mind's eye and to keep that camera rolling as a technique for producing authentic sensory images.

For the first "homework" assignment, students were asked to watch television, which of course immediately sparked their interest. This was followed up with a request to choose a favorite television commercial and write down what images it conveyed (Chapter 2). The next day, students volunteered to share their images with the class, challenging each other to guess what commercial they were describing. By the end of the exercise, everyone agreed that words—and ultimately, writers—*produce* the images.

A subsequent assignment was to read the poem "Baseball" (Reproducible 2:3) and identify the sensory images it conveyed. Groups were then challenged to work together to produce the assigned image "School is a hectic place" (Reproducibles 2:5 & 2:6). Using the rubric charts (Chapter 6 & Appendix), groups were then asked to critique each other's produced images.

Introducing description strategies early in the year, and reinforcing them throughout, trains learners to integrate sensory images into all of their writing pieces. When students, for example, write their personal experience narratives (see "A Cruise Down Memory Lane" in this chapter), I ask them to include at least two appealing sensory images as they did in previous descriptive writing activities. For feedback and follow up, learners again compare and evaluate their images using rubrics like "word choice" and "sentence fluency" to guide them. By this time, students understand the value and power of description within their writing pieces and are ready to take a stab at writing prose or poetry.

Stage 3: The Conference

During conferencing, I meet with students to discuss their accomplishments and challenge areas. It's always important to guard fragile egos before offering ideas or suggesting revisions, but past experience had taught me that with John, it was especially important. On the first day of school, when I invited students to tell me about themselves in their "I'm the one who..." activity (Chapter 1), John wrote of an incident in which he and a friend had egged a child, then laughed and teased the child's angry mother. When I tried to talk with John about the incident (thinking he might be kidding), I discovered his almost paralyzing difficulty—physically and emotionally—with social interaction. A call home, one of many, to learn more about John revealed a rather impatient attitude on his mother's part towards her "difficult" son. My informal conference and call provided further insight into John and his home environment—information that helped me during subsequent conferences.

Stage 4: The Revision Process

I encouraged John to view his first attempt at writing the poem Concerts (Reproducible 4:1) as a "draft" that would benefit from the revision process. I complimented the format of his poem, interpreting what I saw as his application of my workshop lesson on line break in poetry. I also asked John if his alliterative initiation of many lines beginning with "s" words was intentional. He shrugged uncomfortably. I lightheartedly told him he was being modest, hoping to encourage him to complete the piece. I invited him to use my classroom computer. He accepted.

Stage 5: The "Finished" Product

In the rough draft of his poem, John incorporated three of the five senses effectively. This was more than acceptable since I had cautioned students not to use trite or forced images merely for the sake of including all five senses. On his first draft, John crossed out the negative, albeit dramatic, sensory word "stench" and the trite word "fun," demonstrating his commendable willingness and ability to control his images while actively removing the negative or banal. John also attended to mechanical flaws, such as self-correcting the spelling of "you're" to "your."

The defining characteristic of John's revised poem is the pervasive sense of sound. John so quiet; his images loud and deep. His percussive "bass... booming blare of speakers blasting... and skaters crying" inform me that he, indeed, used his "mind's camera" as directed.

John's Brainstorm: The BASS that you can <u>feel</u> a mile away.. STUFF STUFF STUFF Concerts incredibly loud music SMILE :) how do I get home? Why is school so boring?

Concerts (John's First Draft)

Concerts are fun, but the stench
Can be
The bass that can
Start you're heart.
And the booming blare of the
Speakers blasting rookies back
to their cars.
Security guards frightened back to
Unemployment at first sight of the mob of
Punk rockers.
Sociable skaters crying how do
I get home?

Concerts (Revised)

The bass that can start your heart
The booming blare of speakers blasting rookies back
to their cars
Security guards frightened back to unemployment at
first sight of
The mob of punk rockers
Sociable skaters crying how do I get home?

Stage 6: The Assessment

I complimented John's revisions and subtly prodded him to pursue the image he intended. I asked if he meant, "...start your heart *pumping*." He nodded "yes," but chose to retain his more dramatic interpretation: start your heart. The prewriting brainstorm activity told of "incredibly loud music," but his draft commendably produced "the booming blare." I was somewhat disappointed that John relinquished his original line break for one seemingly driven by my computer software's preset margins, but because John so clearly kept his "camera rolling," I wrote only the positive comments on his cover sheet.

Stage 7: The Refined Plan

When John completed his End-of-Quarter Review Sheet (Chapter 6), he was very honest. He wrote that he hated to brainstorm and write rough drafts. When asked how our class could be better, he stated "...if we didn't have to write stories and we didn't have to brainstorm."

Based on his response, I suggested to John that he "think" out the brainstorm and draft stages in his head rather than on paper. He appreciated the respect I gave his introspective prewriting and composing processes. I almost literally held my breath and crossed my fingers as he sat "thinking." By honoring his writing process and preferences, I think John came to respect both his writing and me more. He eventually discovered his writing style and voice, and I discovered that John was a good writer. Though he clearly had not enjoyed self-expressive writing, he demonstrated interest and strong proficiency in each expository and persuasive piece he wrote thereafter, sometimes using

> It is not realistic to believe that all of our students are willing writers in all areas.

the prescribed pre-drafting strategies he hated. He also contributed, albeit quietly, to each oral report, skit, and debate his team produced.

 Think About It

1. Using the rubric chart for writing (Chapter 6 & Appendix), evaluate John's poem.

2. What scores would you assign for word choice, voice, idea/content, and mechanics?

3. How would you justify your evaluation scores?

It is not realistic to believe that all of our students are *willing* writers in all areas. My John was not ready or willing in some ways; yet in other ways, he was. No, he never finished his personal narrative about the "egging" incident that he had briefly, though boldly, shared his first day of school, and I had to encourage him every step of the way to produce his image piece on concerts (Reproducible 4:1). But unless we challenge our students to explore and experience each kind of writing—descriptive, narrative, expository, and persuasive— how else will they discover their strengths and preferences? When we respect our students, their particular areas of interest, their unique abilities and preferences for different kinds of writing and writing processes, we attend to their brain's needs along the way.

Introducing description strategies early in the year, and reinforcing them throughout, trains learners to integrate sensory images into all of their writing pieces.

Upon close examination of John's brainstorm drawing that preceded his writing of "Concerts" (Reproducible 4:1) I noticed a question that shouted volumes. His inner self leaked out in miniscule letters encased in a box: "Why is school so boring?" How do we satisfy the needs of our young learners while we balance curriculum requirements? I admit, it's a challenge, but if we believe that each student has writing strengths that can be developed and if we treat each learner as an individual, we will help shape that reality for them. If we let them know we expect their success and encourage them to expect their own success—even if it is sometimes delayed—then our efforts are not futile. John, like many students, is a more proficient writer today because he was given enough opportunities, encouragement, and accommodation to facilitate his success.

Brain Connection 4-a
Journaling Improves Memory and Cognition

The act of writing down information, scientists know, helps the brain organize and make sense out of complex, multi-faceted pieces of information. Intermittent review of these details increases the probability of retention by the brain in long-term storage. In a recent study, researchers demon-strated that journaling and other forms of notetaking enhance both immediate and long-term recall by providing a written record for later review (Stone, et al. 1998).

Effective journaling, noted Nielsen (1999), engages the mind and the senses in a creative process of "personal story-telling." But she adds that this process does not come immediately; it requires practice. Stone reports that "writ-ing our way through a problem" not only encourages viable solutions to come to the surface naturally, it also helps us to trust and take advantage of our inner thoughts. Journaling is the same process that writers use to develop characters and plot, as well as to overcome "writer's block," Nielsen notes.

In a 12-week study of 702 fifth graders, Hudelson (1997) demonstrated that journaling enhanced both the motivation to read and reading comprehension. Patton and colleagues (1997) found that nursing students who made journal entries on a daily basis improved their critical thinking, observation, and empathy skills.

Audet and colleagues (1996) reported that on-line journaling helped high-school students in advanced physics interact more closely with fellow students, improving their ability to share thoughts and observations, defend viewpoints, and negotiate a group consensus.

Classroom Applications

When students encounter difficulties in the learning process, encourage them to document their thoughts, feelings, and actions in a daily journal. The act of writing their problems down often serves as a welcome catharsis, and later as a form of contemplation to explore viable solutions. Offer to discuss the student's journal entries each week with them if desired. However, since journals are often personal, review entries only when invited to by the student. When multiple students are encountering the same problem, encourage them to meet with each other to discuss their entries, feelings, and processes.

*For full citations, see "References" in Appendix.

Write from the Heart:
Tapping into Personal Experience

"Investing" in the past through our learners' memories is a brain-friendly concept. The more time and effort we invest in helping students recapture memories through words, the stronger their writing foundation will be. Kids are always talking to each other about what happened to them. We can hardly keep them quiet. We need to nudge our students away from the mundane and encourage them to write about experiences stored as long-term memories. To tap into memories worth writing about, help them find the pictures in their minds that are truly "worth a thousand words," then help them transform those pictures into stories worthy of a reading or listening audience.

For kids to write well, we need to help them write about real events, real feelings. We can help them tap into significant memories by taking them on a journey inward to retrieve spark memories. There are many prompts we can use to encourage the recollections of those emotionally laden memories formed in the flash of a moment! We need to ask questions that help students recall memories worth writing about, like hitting a game-winning home run. Then we need to help them convey the exhilarating "crack of that bat" to their reading audience.

The National Board for Professional Teaching Standards believes that accomplished teachers abide by five core propositions*. The first one is this: Teachers are *committed* to their students and learning. This kind of commitment demands that we learn as much about our students as possible. What better way to get to know our students than by inviting them to write about themselves through personal experience narratives? What better way to establish productive and trusting environments than by joining our students in sharing our own personal experience through the same writing exercise?

It is important to share our own writing processes with our students—messy drafts and all—so that they see we take writing seriously and also struggle through drafts before writing final copies. When teacher and learner share the process of writing a personal experience narrative, they build mutual trust and rapport. When I, for example, share my frightening night-dive experience with my students, they realize I trust them enough to describe how scared I was when "I heard what sounded like Godzilla's footsteps crushing Tokyo!" In return, they start to trust me with their feelings, their fears, their stories.

When we teach grammatical conventions in context—through writing—we "provide added value": We help students learn *not* for the short term (e.g., the test), but for life. When writing is meaningful to students,

*See the appendix for a list of all five core propositions, reprinted by permission from the National Board for Professional Teaching Standards.

all aspects of it—including grammar—become meaningful. They *want* to know about nouns and verbs and adjectives, not because it helps them get a good grade, but because it helps them become good writers.

A Cruise Down Memory Lane— Writing the Personal Experience Narrative

The brain is a natural born storyteller! We just need to prompt learners to take a trip down "Memory Lane" where the heart of personal experience resides.

Learning Activity: *"Memory Lane"*

Instructions:

◆ Have students read and discuss several examples of personal experience narratives, focusing on (1) how and why the authors might have chosen the specific episodes they did to write about, and (2) the precise nouns, verbs, adjectives, dialogue, etc. the authors used.

◆ Give students the "Memory Lane" brainstorm sheet (Reproducible 4:2a) while projecting or using Reproducible 4:2b to guide the discussion.

◆ Once learners have generated and discussed possible topics, ask them to think about the memories a bit more. What particular event stands out in their minds? Students often list things like "When my parents got a divorce" as a sad event*; however, when probed you find out they remember *that* it happened but not a *specific occurrence*.

◆ After brainstorming a list of possible topics to write about, ask students to choose one to expound upon for their narrative**.

◆ Review, discuss, and implement various grammatical conventions throughout the narrative unit in context to students' writing.

*The topic of divorce holds a strong potential for poetry. See Appendix for a student writing sample on the topic of "divorce."
**I ask students to review their list and narrow it to the one or two topics that inspire the mental pictures they really want to share. These memories need not be traumatic, although they often are.

Memory Lane
Brainstorm Sheet

The memories of_____

Your name here

✏ _____

✏ _____

✏ _____

✏ _____

✏ _____

✏ _____

✏ _____

✏ _____

✏ _____

✏ _____

✏ _____

✏ _____

✏ _____

✏ _____

✏ _____

✏ _____

✏ _____

✏ _____

Teacher Tip:
As you proceed through the "Memory Lane" activity, encourage students to *fill* this worksheet with memories, thus generating a list of possible topics on which to write. Suggest they write words or phrases that provide a cue for each memory (e.g., sad—the day my dog died). Encourage your students to refer to the list throughout this year to generate topics for all kinds of writing.

Memory Lane

From the following cues, write single words or whole phrases that you remember (e.g., sad...the day my dog died). You can write your responses on the brainstorm sheet provided.

My journey may recall a time I was:

☞ Frightened

☞ Happy

☞ Sad

☞ Lonely

☞ Angry

☞ Excited

☞ Mischievous

My journey may recall:

☞ A prized possession

☞ A time of year

☞ An achievement

☞ A situation

☞ A birthday

☞ A hobby

☞ A sport

My journey may involve a memory based on:

☞ A sight

☞ A scent

☞ A sound

☞ A taste

☞ A touch

Teacher Tip:
Display the above prompts with an overhead projector. Show one line at a time, covering the rest with a piece of paper. Encourage as much sharing as possible. Some students may wish to keep the memories on their brainstorm sheet private without comment, while others will jump at the opportunity to share aloud. This activity can take a full class period of 40 minutes or more. However, the volume of meaningful discussion generated by it makes it well worth the time. It is important for you to share your own memories too, especially if students find any of the cues too abstract at first (e.g., a scent). If you want students to share, you must share.

More Memories

Do any of the following activities spark a memory for you?

- Acting
- Archery
- Baby-sitting
- Badminton
- Baseball
- Basketball
- Board Games
- Boating
- Bowling
- Camping
- Cheerleading
- Dentist
- Diving
- Fishing
- Football
- Golf
- Hiking
- Hockey
- Horseback Riding
- Hunting
- Ice Hockey
- Jogging
- Music Playing/Listening
- Painting
- Photography
- Rollerblading
- Rollerskating
- Skiing
- Snowboarding
- Softball
- Summer Camp
- Swimming
- Tennis
- Walking
- Waterskiing
- Wrestling
- What Else????

Teacher Tip:
Add more activities to the list as kids volunteer them. Believe me, they will notice what's been forgotten.

Stay Tuned

My own teaching unit that involves personal experience narratives begins with reading stories that range
from standing up to a bully (*A Precocious
Autobiography* by Yevgeny Yevtushenko) and hating a
guacamole green jacket (*The Jacket* by Gary Soto) to
mourning the loss of a grandfather (a student's work).
Use a prompt (Reproducible 4:2) to stimulate memories that will feed students' stories. Have them recall
the people involved, the details they see in their mind,
and at least one quote they "hear" ringing in their ears.

As you draft your own personal experience narrative,
you'll model the process for learners. I also conduct a
role-play exercise whereby students learn how to critique the work of others in a productive and non-
offensive fashion (Chapter 5). Modeling conference
protocol in the workshop format teaches learners how
to give and receive feedback while also helping them
make neural connections between writing and writing etiquette.

As the drafts of their work progress, learners help
assess their own and each other's writing, using conference questions like the following: What seems to
be the best or strongest part of my story? What seems
to be boring or unnecessary? Can any part be revised
or deleted to make the story stronger? What suggestions do you have for my story?

Once students have written a number of drafts, we
discuss the revision process. I share a series of student
samples from past years that clearly demonstrate revision suggestions with arrows connecting text to
margin notes, cross outs, whole sections of text deleted or moved for strength, and queries to the author.
Students are required to revise at least one portion of
their drafts—even if they opt for the original version
later on.

Brain Connection 4-b
Three Steps to Effective Task Learning

Comprehension increases when students receive a visual demonstration of a new learning task followed by a verbal explanation of it from another and cemented with a reiteration of the technique in the learner's own words, suggests a new study (Crowley & Siegler 1999). The most important link in this learning scenario may not necessarily be the observation itself, but the observation followed by an explanation from another and the self-explanation, which allows learners to analyze and internalize the information in multiple modalities.

Scientists know that when we observe or read something, increased activity occurs in the left-frontal, temporal, occipital, and parietal lobes of the brain—key areas that search for meaning, patterns, and context in what we see. Scientists are also aware that without meaning, there is no learning.

Crowley and Siegler (ibid) studied the problem-solving strategies of 34 kindergartners, 40 first-graders, and 40 second-graders in a tic-tac-toe computer game. The children who were most effective at comprehending and employing new strategies were those who observed the effective techniques of other players followed by a verbal explanation from them, and cemented with a reiteration of the technique in the learner's own words.

Brain Connection 4-b continued...

The Crowley-Siegler study demonstrates that a verbal explanation or validation of what has been observed provides the brain the chance to make sense out to what has been seen. In other words, it allows the brain to make the necessary neural connections for meaningful learning to occur.

 ## Classroom Applications

This research affirms the importance of critique sessions, peer learning, and conferencing explains why it is helpful for students to review other's writing samples before embarking on their own. Invite students to reflect, discuss, and write about the strong and weak characteristics they observe in other writing models. Always encourage explanations (and questions) from learners about what they've seen and heard. Strengthen neural connections with the 3-step process of observing, listening, and asking for an explanation in the learner's own words. This process also represents an excellent way to prepare learners for writing assessment tests.

*For full citations, see "References" in Appendix.

Practice Always Precedes Perfection

Practice does not necessarily make "perfect," but it always precedes perfection. As students mature, they gradually come to understand that revising their work is an essential step in producing clear and accurate writing. I show learners my many sloppy drafts with multiple cross outs and arrows. They see that it is normal for writers to think messy and write messy during the composing stage when the brain is tapping into multiple and diverse memory pathways—searching and creating and revising. Learning to write well requires practice—lots of it!

As the days progress, I ask learners to place stars next to at least two examples of descriptive language, vivid actions, or dialogue, depending on the focus of the day's lesson. Daily lessons are based on student needs, which are identified during writing and conference times. Some lessons address mechanics (e.g., paragraphing main ideas, structuring dialogue, and punctuation in dialogue), while others prompt writing (e.g., write four lines of dialogue that may work to recapture an idea or the gist of your story). I encourage my students not to bring their works-in-progress home, however, reminding them I get paid to coach them through the process, not to grade papers after the fact.

> "Fake it until you make it."
> —*Anonymous*

Make it clear to students how they will be graded on a day-to-day basis during the writing process. My students know that the group-work rubric (Chapter 6 & Appendix), which they all have, is my primary grading reference. To help encode the grading criteria in their memory, I share former students' personal experience narratives—partial and whole, with names removed—for us to critique as a group in class. "Playing" teacher creates a wonderful brain-compatible work setting that learners enthusiastically take on. Using the group-work and rubrics to determine work quality, we/they evaluate and grade the anonymous narratives. How can we expect learners to achieve our dreams for them if they don't know exactly what they are?

Meet Chase: "There Goes the Trailer!"

My student, Chase, was little in stature and big in heart. It was easy to gain an idea of his personality from the ideas he wrote on his "Memory Lane" brainstorm sheet (e.g., mischievous: "TP = cops" [wrapping toilet paper around a neighbor's yard and getting caught]; sensitive: "sad = grandpa" [dying]).

Information gathered from the "Getting to Know You" activity (Reproducible 1:2) conducted on the first day of class reinforced my understanding of Chase. Chase was predominately a kinesthetic and social learner. His "I'm the one who..." response confessed that he felt bad when he made his brother cry about his braces and that he liked to throw rocks, which got him into trouble. Not surprisingly, Chase chose as his first piece, a camping trip with his friend's family in which their trailer unhitched after his friend's dad momentarily lost control of their car.

Chase's narrative applied all of the lessons I had addressed in class, especially the very important lesson on revision, which helped him remove much of the "breakfast-to-dinner" recitation that appeared in his first draft. When I had asked him about the real story he wished to share he replied, "When we lost the trailer." He worked hard to cut the superfluous, to retell the crux of the story. Here's a "sound byte" from "There Goes the Trailer," which recounts the unexpected mishap:

...We were driving around a turn and all of a sudden we heard his dad shout, "Oh my God, oh my lord! Why does this have to happen to me?" Everyone looked up in a hurry, frightened, and started yelling, "What happened? What? What?" No response. We looked back behind the car: "Where's the trailer?"...

Journeying down "Memory Lane" fuels our creative engines and keeps the writer's head, heart, and hand moving. Students willingly learn because they want to write down their stories. Each new application or genre helps them absorb more about the art of writing. The personal experience journey gets them kick-started with what all of us know best—ourselves.

Before you ask students to do this assignment, write at least one personal experience narrative yourself. You may wish to maintain a journal with reflections on the experience as you draft and revise your work. This process will help you encode the knowledge and connections necessary for effectively coaching others through the process.

Crossing the Great Curriculum Divide

Sometimes we are assigned to teach outside of our expertise: This doesn't have to be a bad thing. My own experience during a year of teaching a section of seventh-grade science showed me that crossing curricula without abandoning language arts was possible. Each quarter, I met a new class of students whom I was to teach about the systems of the human body. Here's how I approached the task.

I explained to the class, which was divided into groups of five or six students each, that they were working for my multimedia corporation. Each of the groups was asked to come up with an idea for a health magazine or a television show whose focus was, of course, good heath. I asked each group to choose a name for their magazine or TV show. I directed them to create advertisements, a feature article, or a TV show episode about the various human body systems they needed to know. You may be wondering how they could embark on such an endeavor when they hadn't even learned about the systems yet.

The first thing they were naturally interested in deciding was whether they were going to represent a television or magazine; did they want to write a TV script or feature article? I asked students to bring in their favorite magazines or taped episodes/clips from talk shows they might like to model. The homework response was virtually 100 percent.

"The brightest students are the ones who always have their hands in the air to expand the discussion through stories about their own experience: They unconsciously maintain and extend their own memory networks through active recall. It's as if their brains know how important it is for them to act on their knowledge and beliefs, to not sit passively by and let their classmates make all of the mental connections."

—*Robert Sylwester*

Rather than force them to open their science books, read, review, and test for the short-term memory haul, I trusted learners to make choices for themselves. They eventually and naturally sought textual information to complete their assignments. Textbooks never open faster than when students work within media production deadlines. And, when they open textbooks or surf Websites on their own volition, memory pathways open up for the long haul.

In planning for this new unit, I first had to consider what it was about the human body I wanted students to learn. How would they demonstrate their acquired knowledge and understanding? Whether they chose to write a feature article or to replicate a talk show, I determined students needed to (1) identify five or more parts of each system, (2) name the pathways and interrelationships of each system, and (3) suggest the causes and consequences of damage to each system.

It worked: The unit was very successful. Groups met the challenge with great aplomb. One of the talk shows I especially liked, for example, depicted the host interviewing a cardiologist along with Mr. Heart and Ms. Cholesterol. With a little imagination and a lot of attention to brain-compatible concepts, it is clear that diverse curriculum objectives can be met in engaging ways. Dialogue with learners to create the direction, format, and evaluation criteria. In this way students become active shareholders in their own learning process. Ask them how they might like to learn, and they will choose to learn because you make learning fun.

Let's suppose, for example, that you're working with a history teacher who is currently teaching about Harriet Tubman and her Underground Railroad. How might you incorporate this content with personal experience narratives (or whatever kind of writing you're facilitating) to bridge curricula and increase neural pathways of real learning?

Here's one idea:
Pretend you are a runaway slave who was saved by Harriet Tubman. Write about your personal experience with Harriet Tubman. Create a story that includes details and dialogue that demonstrate your understanding of this great historical figure.

Think About It

1. Can you think of some engaging writing prompts that relate to your own specific curriculum?

2. Can you think of some prompts that cross your particular grade level's language-arts and science curriculums?

3. How do cross-curricular activities support brain-compatible principles?

Cross-curriculum writing prompts that ask students to create fictional episodes around real characters solder new memory connections between various content areas and writing. The more we help kids manipulate new information, the more we help them build and strengthen existing neural connections. There's no limit to the connections possible.

Here's a math story prompt, for example: Imagine an algebraic equation. Pretend that you are X, the unknown value on one side of the equation. Write the personal experience narrative of your journey to discover your identity. Let your creativity go...The connections are endless and fun to create!

To the brain, playing is synonymous with learning. Games, whether played in or out of the classroom, ignite the imagination as the complexity of life is explored in a familiar, nonthreatening, and ultimately entertaining environment. When the mind relaxes, motivation, learning, and creativity multiply as new ideas are generated. Game playing also enhances problem-solving and organizational skills while engaging emotions and helping the brain to lock in new memory. There's no doubt about it, when it comes to learning, playing is serious business.

Think about the instruction manuals that accompany the highly sophisticated video games kids habitually play. Youngsters read every word of these complex documents willingly and repeatedly because they are motivated—motivated to master the game, to win. The naturally curious brain seeks to learn and work hard *when motivated*. Therefore, our challenge as educators is to create a setting that *inspires* learners to learn and that engages the complete mind/body system. The following Real-Life Application is just one of many ways we can achieve this very realistic teaching goal.

 ### Real-Life Application:
Hero Quest—The Serious Business of
Playing (nonfiction/essays)

Hero Quest is an adventure game that extends learners' enthusiasm for playing to the hard work of writing an essay. The prize for those who prevail in *Hero Quest* is a cohesive organization of ideas critical to expository/essay writing.

Hero Quest represents a powerful tool for mapping out a writing plan or outline. Used in or beyond the language arts classroom, its visual graphic orientation is especially helpful for predominantly visual learners. Planning a response visually provides many learners with a sense of security. They draw a head and think about what they want to say; they draw a torso and understand that a solidly constructed body of support is necessary; they draw the legs and are reminded to ground their responses with a conclusion. For many learners, *Hero Quest* becomes their organizational strategy of choice once they've experienced success with it.

The game is simple: Students identify a "hero" or favorite character from an assigned or chosen reading. With colored markers, they draw a graphic representation of their hero and apply pertinent characteristics.

Some students will prefer to draw their own hero figure outline, others may choose a pre-printed version (Reproducible 4:4). Either way, ultimately, their heroes will represent an effectively organized essay outline.

Organization is one of the critical rubrics used to assess proficiency in writing. It's recognized as such by groups as small as local school districts and as large as The Nation's Report Card people, NAEP (National Assessment for Educational Progress).

Unit Summary

Objectives:
◆ Students learn to construct an organized outline that guides their subsequent essay writing.
◆ Students develop expository writing skills across disciplines. This version of the game focuses on outlining and writing an essay in response to a literary work—a typical language arts objective nationwide. However, it can easily be adapted to any other content area, as well.

Age Appropriateness:
This unit, as presented, is designed for sixth through ninth graders of any skill level; however, it is an especially effective tool for learners with a visual-spatial learning-style preference and for struggling readers/writers. With a little modification, the unit can be customized for other age groups, as well.

Materials and Resources:
◆ Activity sheets, a teacher's guide, overhead transparencies, and student samples.

Methodology:

◆ Teacher facilitated whole- and small-group instruction. Students can work alone, in pairs, and/or in cooperative groups.

◆ Student's responses can be written directly onto a teacher-tailored *Hero Quest* outline (Reproducible 4:4) or on the student's own hero outline. (Monitor this stage closely: Kids tend to draw figures too small to contain outline content.)

◆ Students compose essays based on their completed outlines that contain an introduction, body, and conclusion.

The Plan:

◆ Provide learners with a reading choice from a number of appropriate options. The following example is based on the reading of an abridged version of *The Fall of the House of Usher* by Edgar Allen Poe.

◆ Distribute copies of the *Hero Quest* instructions and outline sheet. Use visually oriented handouts or overheads to review the instructions as a class before getting started.

◆ Facilitate both whole-group instruction and individual teacher/student assistance while the game plays out and outlines are constructed. Facilitate conferences between various drafts of the outline and essay.

One Student's *Hero Quest* drawing.

Your Noble Quest for a Hero

Before your adventure begins, think about the characters you want to have join you in your quest. Identify at least four characters and write their names in the area provided below. Also include the name of the book or movie that inspired each character. One of your characters will join you in your ultimate "Hero Quest."

Character	Where did you meet this character?
1.	1.
2.	2.
3.	3.
4.	4.

Once you've named four characters, discuss their traits and characteristics with other learners. Why did you choose these characters? Why do you admire them? Is there anything about them that you don't like? What? Why did your classmates choose their specific characters?

_____

_____

_____

_____

_____

_____

_____

_____

The Quest

You've identified at least four characters for your upcoming adventure. You've read about them in a book or gotten to know them in a movie. But at the moment, they are trapped in the strange world of "Vague"—a make-believe land where they're vanishing because everything is so terribly vague.

The good news is there's still time to save your characters. So far, only their arms have faded to a blur. Your quest is to rescue <u>one</u> hero from the world of "Vague." To do this you must retrieve his/her arms. Once you rescue your main character, he/she will be able to save the others.
Good luck with your mission!

Rescuing Your Main Character

✏ Using either your own hero outline or the one provided, write the name of your main character—the one you wish to rescue—in the head area of your hero.

✏ Write the title of the book or movie where you first met this character directly below his/her name.

Notes:_____

_____

_____

_____

_____

_____

Your Hero Quest Figure

Tattooing Your Hero

As you enter the world of "Vague" where the vanishing body parts are secretly stored, find your character's arms. <u>Be careful!</u> Each arm has a quality tattooed on it! If you don't select the tattoos that best describe the personality of your hero, his or her arms will vanish once again! If you discover the quality you want is not listed here, great! You're thinking creatively. Go ahead and create your own tattoo.

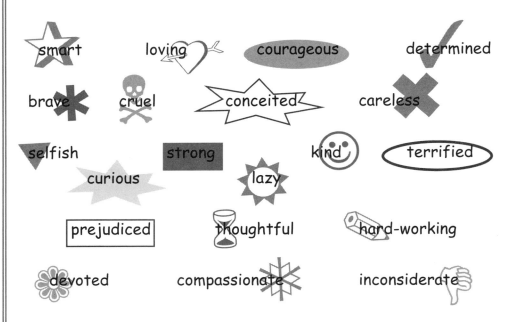

smart   loving   courageous   determined

brave   cruel   conceited   careless

selfish   strong   kind   terrified

curious   lazy

prejudiced   thoughtful   hard-working

devoted   compassionate   inconsiderate

✏ Defend your choices! In order to succeed, think about what your character has done that demonstrates his or her unique qualities. Write some phrases or statements that support your choices in your hero's body area. Do not proceed to the next step until you <u>know</u> that you can defend any challenges against your statements. Otherwise, you jeopardize the mission!

✏ Once you have successfully secured your character's arms, write his/her tattooed traits in the head area of your hero, as well.

Legs to Stand On

Congratulations...Your character is almost free to leave the strange world of "Vague." If the qualities you've chosen are accurate and can be defended, your hero will survive. However, before your hero can be released from the land of "Vague," he or she needs legs to stand on.

✏ To do this, restate the information in the head of your hero to his or her legs. Once this is done, you will have completed your first quest! Congratulations! The next step is to use the hero you've created to construct an essay outline.

Here's a visual example of the steps described:

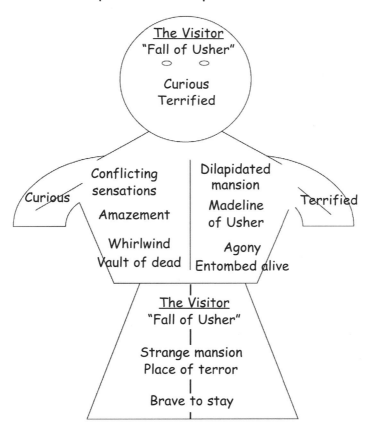

This example was created by a seventh grader in response to an abridged (grade-level appropriate) version of Poe's classic, *The Fall of the House of Usher*.

Your Hero Writes

Now, to transform your hero into an essay, follow the steps below:

✏ Write an introduction that states the purpose of your essay. To do this, ask yourself a central question to prompt a response. For example, the student writer in "The Fall of the House of Usher" asked, why was the visitor afraid?

✏ Next, "arm" your essay thesis with sentences that support your hero's tattooed personality traits.

✏ Finally, write a conclusion that restates the essay's purpose. "Stand" your essay on solid ground by restating your introduction. You can include an opinion you expressed about the topic in your conclusion, but avoid using the firstperson voice.

Essay Introduction Example:

The Visitor in *The Fall of the House of Usher* finds that his intense curiosity for a dilapidated mansion leads him into a Tomb of Terror.

Pretending can be fun and can help you learn! Whenever you prepare to write an essay, "play" a version of *Hero Quest*: Give life to your outline! Change the objectives of your quest to fit each essay's requirements. Draw your armless hero and recreate the game to fit the needs of the assigned essay—pretend a creature from "Vague" is challenging you to prove yourself "essay" worthy!

For a different perspective on the art of writing, read other peoples' essays and think about the *Hero Quest* process in reverse. For example, ask, What was the writer's mission or the essay's purpose? What traits did the author "tattoo" the characters with? How does the author justify his or her choices?

Other Students Write...

The four student hero outlines and essays that follow demonstrate the versatility and effectiveness of the *Hero Quest* approach to organization. You'll notice that the subjects range from science to social studies. Essay 1 is well organized and demonstrates a grasp of essay technique. Essay 2, in contrast, demonstrates that students sometimes write solid outlines but fail to apply the outlines to their essays. Essay 3 demonstrates how revisions are an important step in the process of producing a clearly written and well-organized finished product. And, Essay 4, while exhibiting solid scientific knowledge, demonstrates gaps in essay organization and technique.

Hero Quest can help teachers identify gaps in understanding and application before a student succumbs to a sense of failure or frustration. Regardless of subject matter, we can help students avoid potentially flawed writing and revel in exceptionally good writing with guidance in the conception stage. What better way to authentically pre-assess students' writing than by "seeing the whole picture"—from their point of view—before the student starts writing.

Essay 1:
Justine's Hero Quest

Would you stay in a house if you thought "the Bony Hand of Death" was heading for it? The visitor in "The Fall of the House of Usher" by Edgar A. Poe did just that! In many ways the visitor proved to the reader he was full of fear. Yet, in spite of his fear of the house and the people in it, he stayed with his friend, Roderick Usher.

The Visitor
"Fall of Usher"
Fear
House
People

Servants
Ghost-like
Fear People
Madeline
More alive when dead

Spooky house
Eye-like windows
Fear House
Vault/Tomb
Bony hand

The Visitor
"Fall of Usher"
House
Scary people
Brave to stay

The house of Usher was no ordinary house. The visitor told about its "vacant eyelike window" which made the house seem real. He was really afraid when he discovered they buried family members right there in the house. He was even more afraid when he discovered that chamber was right underneath the room where he stayed!

Not only did the house frighten the visitor, its "tenants" did too. When he looked at Lady Madeline after she had died, she looked more alive in her coffin than when she was alive. He also thought she was a ghost when he first saw her because she moved so oddly; she would move, stand still a long while and then move again. After Usher dies and the visitor tries to give orders to the servants, they ignore him. He was so afraid, he was convinced he was the only living thing in the house.

The visitor in "The Fall of the House of Usher" was full of fear. Not just because of the house but the people too. He was very brave for staying in the house in spite of his fear. Not too many people would do that.

Reproduced as written by student, including errors.

Essay 2:
Clayton's Hero Quest

This essay is about the story, "The Fall of the House of Usher." The main character was the visitor. Other characters were Lady Madeline and Roderick Usher.

The visitor was loyal to his friend to stay even though he thought that everyone was a ghost.

The visitor was brave because his room was above the burial chamber. He was also brave because he thought that the house was haunted and everyone in it as well.

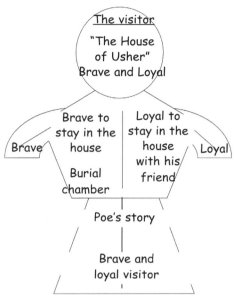

The visitor
"The House of Usher"
Brave and Loyal

Brave — Brave to stay in the house — Loyal to stay in the house with his friend — Loyal

Burial chamber

Poe's story

Brave and loyal visitor

In conclusion Lady Madeline dies supposedly and so does Roderick. The visitor got on his horse and rode off he looked back and he saw the house fall apart.

Note:

Although, this student did not follow his *Hero Quest* outline, the good news is that remedial action is far easier because he wrote a marginal but adequate outline. I would point out that the introductions don't match, and that Clayton's essay introduction reads more like a plot summary! The two body paragraphs have potential but are not developed. The last paragraph, like the first, succumbs to the problematic student habit of writing a plot summary, rather than an essay.

I would encourage a consolidation of the two qualities into one—loyalty being the more effective, since the visitor's bravery is the causal effect of his loyalty. Focusing on loyalty will also help the student develop the body paragraph. Next, the teacher can encourage the student to revise the essay and check it against the outline to ensure that they match.

Reproduced as written by student, including errors.

Meet Alvaro

The next example (Reproducible 4:10) demonstrates the effectiveness of the *Hero Quest* approach with nonnative English speakers. In this case, students chose from a number of prompts to complete a district writing-assessment test based on a literary selection. As per typical state guidelines, the essay needed to satisfy specific rubrics in writing. Each student received the rubric chart and was directed to assess his or her own draft against the rubric chart before peer conferencing. The test was administered the last week of the second quarter.

Alvaro was mainstreamed into my classroom from his ESL class after 6 weeks of school. An extremely polite and respectful young man, he sought and welcomed the opportunity to be in an English-speaking class. Alvaro's mechanical skills were commendable for a newly mainstreamed ESL student. In simple yet eloquent English, he presented strong evidence that he could read literature critically and interpretively. His written work at testing time, however, did not reflect his oral ability.

I served as Alvaro's conference partner during the essay test. After reading his draft about the boy and mother from *Sounder*, I recognized that he had written a plot summary that included episodes from the movie, not the book version of the story. When I examined his *Hero Quest* outline I could not understand much of it, so I asked him to read it to me while I corrected the misspelled words. Through this process, I realized that his outline *did* address the prompt as it related to the book, and it clearly demonstrated a commendable analysis of the *Sounder* character. I praised Alvaro and coached him to write another draft, this time one that followed his well-prepared outline.

After conferencing with Alvaro, he wrote a similar, neater (bless his heart) version of the original draft. At this point, I remained patient and resolved. I accepted that I might not have communicated with him effectively. I risked speaking in the limited Spanish I was learning since joining an ESL team of teachers. I balanced the benefit of better comprehension against the risk of insulting Alvaro. He was proud of being in an English-speaking classroom, and I wasn't sure how he would take it. When I began speaking in Spanish, his eyes grew sorrowful, but he listened intently nonetheless. I told him, through words and gestures, to try again—to follow his good outline. To simplify the assignment, I told him to write only on the courage of the boy,  rather than on both the boy and the mother, which would require more examples. I also told him it was okay to use examples from the movie, as well as the book, since Alvaro had mentioned he'd really enjoyed the movie version.

The outline includes my revisions after conferencing with Alvaro. I wrote the reminder about a conclusion and added the arrow to visually help him.

Essay Prompt:

Sometimes love and courage help people to survive when terrible things happen to them. The mother and son in "Sounder" survive the horrors of racism because of their love and courage. In a well-constructed essay, describe how the mother and the son showed their love and courage. Be sure to use specific examples from the novel to support your answer.

Essay 3:
Alvaro's Hero Quest

Alvaro's work is based on the story *Sounder*, a teenage classic written by William Armstrong. It follows a loving family of sharecroppers determined to survive the racism of their time after the father is imprisoned for 6 years for stealing food to feed his family.

Sounder
boy

love and courage

He stands up against racism because they ignored it. When the guard put hole in the cake, he did nothing.

When the boy was looking for his father the guy from the jail hit him. The boy ran away.

Don't forget to restate your essay's purpose.

First Draft:

One day the father went to work and he disappeared. Nobody from his family knew what or where he has gone. His son went to look for him and found a jail. When the guard looked at him the guard hit him and chased the boy away. After all that the boy found a school. The teacher told him to come in. She was very nice. After school was over the teacher gave him a book and the boy took it home. The boy told his mother. The next day they were working on the farm when Sounder returned and everybody was happy. Then the boy heard someone screaming. He noticed that it was his dad. They were all happy. The next day the boy's father wanted to take him shopping, and the boy didn't want to go. Since that day they were living happy....

Reproduced as written by student, including errors.

Note: Spelling corrections have been made in the following example for ease of reading:

Alvaro's Essay Revision

The boy from Sounder showed his courage. He ignored other people that were making fun of him. The boy was always good to other people but the other kids were not good to him. When he found the school one boy told a story of other kids, and they just laughed at him. The boy stood up for him. He said that he believed what he said.

Another way that the boy showed courage was when he was taking the cake to his father and the guard pushed holes in the cake and the boy ignored this.

Alvaro's final draft successfully recounted three incidents (two from the book and one from the movie) that demonstrated the boy's courage.

Hero Quest clearly assisted Alvaro and continues to assist ESL students and other challenged learners who benefit from a clear road map—navigating them away from plot summaries and towards original responses.

Reproduced as written by student, including errors.

Writing Prompt: How is science related to the arts?

Essay 4:
Sandy's Essay

I believe science, art, writing, and creativity are very much related to each other in many ways. In this essay I will show you how they are related and why. I will talk about famous people like Leonardo DeVinci, Darwin, Copernicus, and Kepler, who used all of these skills to make a break-through in technology. So, sit back and enjoy!

Science, writing, and creativity are related. Creativity relates to everything because all great things start with an idea, like Copernicus and his idea that the Earth revolved around the sun and not the other way around. Gallileo was also very creative and attempted each time something was proven, to investigate the claim to find out if it was true himself.

Art, for many scientists, helps paint the picture of the solution, or in some cases, the problem. DeVinci drew the first pictures of cirrhosis of the liver, as well as muscles, blood vessels, and nerves in the arms. His whole study of the human body was inspired by his perfectionism in art and his need for his sculptures to be perfect. But still many people use art as a way of showing information and facts, like Copernicus showed his thought that the Earth moved around the sun.

Writing is also part of the big picture. All mankind throughout history has written his thoughts, ideas, notes, accomplishments, and much, much more in order to remember. All scientists write down their findings and later on go back, relate similarities, compare differences and come up with a solution. Many people also write down their findings in the books to share with others the information they have acquired, like Kepler and his book, "The New Astronomy" on how Mars made an elliptical orbit. Even Darwin's grandfather, Erasmus Darwin, wrote a long poem on his work as a physician.

In conclusion, I hope you now see that science relates to writing, art, and creativity in many ways. We write things down in order to remember, compare, and contrast our findings. Writing is a vital necessity to science and life. Art is related to science in the way that some things are better drawn and can paint the picture for the reader in a way that words cannot. Creativity is related to science because all ideas start out as creativity. I hope you now agree with me that science, art, writing, and creativity all relate to each other in one way or another.

Note:
Although Sandy's essay demonstrates a sound understanding of science content, it could benefit from an organizational revision. As a writing teacher how might you work with this student to help her strengthen the essay's organization?

Brain Connection 4-c
Reflection Aids Learning

Research suggests that a healthy dose of reflection and/or rest after meaningful learning may be just what the brain needs to process new information, strengthen neural connections, and deepen consolidation (Frank & Greenberg 1994; Frydenberg 1991; Hasselmo 1999; Karni 1994).

In a study of 88 fifth- and sixth-graders, Shafir and Eagle (1995) found that students who spent periods in self-reflection after learning were not only better learners and problem-solvers, but developed better corrective strategies than subjects who did not reflect.

Scientist know that CREB, a protein in the brain that is known to facilitate long-term memory in REM (rapid eye movement) sleep, also plays a major role in consolidating long-term learning in mental reflection. CREB binds with serotonin, a neurotransmitter that regulates such functions as relaxation and sleep, aiding in long-term declarative memories concerning facts, ideas, and images (Hasselmo 1999).

Physiological evidence supports a two-stage model of the encoding process in which the initial encoding occurs during active waking and deeper consolidation occurs via the formation of additional memory traces during quiet waking (down time) or slow-wave sleep (ibid).

Classroom Applications

Disseminate content in bite-size chunks. Give kids meaningful projects that encourage reflection. Follow up new learning with classroom discussions or "solve the problem" case studies. Embed mechanical lessons (e.g. grammar, vocabulary, spelling, word usage, technique, fluency) into larger assignments. In other words, integrate semantic learning into real-life contexts and give kids the opportunity to reflect on their personal strengths and correct their weaknesses. Have students evaluate their own work and that of their peers (See Rubrics; Chapter 6 & Appendix).

*For full citations, see "References" in Appendix.

Drawing a Kinesthetic Connection

Hero Quest represents just one of many organizing tools! Rather than force students to use a particular organizing strategy, introduce a number of them and let learners decide which is most suitable for their particular needs.

One way to help predominately kinesthetic learners use and remember the steps involved in the *Hero Quest* adventure is to lead a verbally guided exercise that attaches movements to the game. For example, you might suggest that learners sit at a desk or table and think about standing up. Say, "Don't actually do it! Just *think* about it. In your mind, picture how you plan to stand up. Will you press both hands to the desk to support you? Will you twist around in your seat or slide out from the side?"

"Now that you've thought about it, go ahead and stand up. You've just mimicked the effective organization of an essay! You thought about what it was you were going to do, you considered the support you would need, and then you did it. You stood yourself on solid ground."

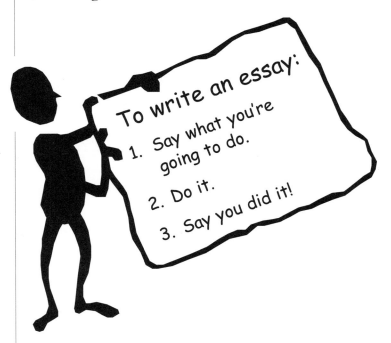

To write an essay:
1. Say what you're going to do.
2. Do it.
3. Say you did it!

Dr. Carol Kessner, an inspiring graduate school professor I once had, shared some valuable advice about writing a thesis that I've repeated to students many times. *"Say what you're going to do, do it, then say you did it."* Whether you're writing a few pages or a complete dissertation, the advice holds true.

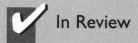 In Review

1. What brain principles are important for meeting the cognitive and emotional needs of children like John?

2. What do you know about brain-compatible writing so far?

3. What brain principles are applicable to the "Write from the Heart" (personal experience narratives) example described in this chapter?

4. Why is the "Hero Quest" adventure considered a brain-friendly strategy for teaching essay writing?

*R*eady, Set, Rehearsal

Show Me How to Show You

Then I broke my arm...
There are a lot of animals in Africa....
We went to the beach...

Have you ever felt like you were reading a shopping list when reviewing students' writing? Almost all of us have mistakenly believed that we are helping the students who penned such work when we say to them, "Show me, don't tell me." But if students' writing is vague or trite, it may be because our instructions are vague or trite. Upon hearing the directive, show me, don't tell me, kids should rightfully reply, "Okay... Show me how to show you!"

To show learners what you mean by writing with precision, challenge them to identify, underline, and revise vague words and phrases. When Katie writes, for example, "I broke my arm," ask her what exactly happened when she hurt her arm? When she says, "My arm twisted as it stretched out to block my face from hitting the concrete," affirm her ability to recall the vivid details of the experience and ask her to put it down on paper in the same way. Leading students through the process of composing *shows* them that they have the words to write a good story. When Joey writes, "There are lots of animals in Africa," ask him what kind of animals and where in Africa? If his only responses are "elephants" and "the desert," he needs to put on his sleuthing cap and investigate the topic further. Ask him to discover an African animal that he has never heard of before and identify the country in which it lives. Ask him to describe what makes it unique in the animal kingdom.

Writing Is Revising...Is Revising...Is Revising

How can we get learners to work at finding an exact word, an accurate phrase, or a precise sentence to make their writing shine? How do we convey that

revision is an essential step in that process? As brain-compatible writing teachers, we need to help learners relinquish first-draft ideas without relinquishing their self-esteem. It is critical for students to learn that writing is not merely an act of putting words down on paper, but a process of brainstorming, conceptualizing, drafting, and revising, revising, revising! Moving learners through this often tedious process can be trying... and exhilarating! When resistance happens, I practice affirming my three core beliefs about teaching:

The first core belief is that every student is good at some kind of writing, so I never give up on them—even the difficult ones, even the learners who resist every attempt to help them. They all eventually find a genre in which to showcase their voice. In the process, I provide them with both written and verbal congratulatory comments to harness and build on even their tiniest of successes.

Second, I practice patience. Criticizing students' efforts when they just don't seem to "get it" only causes them to retreat from their learning cortexes and default to their emotional midbrain where the chemical chowder of self-defense abides. It may even stimulate their fight or flight response, losing them completely to misbehavior or indifference. Instead, I emphasize that writing is revising... is revising... is revising. It takes a lot of patience. I let them know that we writers need to be our own best (and worst) critics. And I let them know that we are all in this game of writing together. Yes, we brain-compatible writing teachers work hard—another reason why incorporating fun into our classrooms is essential.

Third, I avoid sarcasm, which robs learners of the trusting bond they need to have with their teachers. I do not confuse humor with sarcasm. A thousand times, Yes! to humor, but sarcasm is too often insidiously veiled verbal abuse labeled "just kidding." Sarcasm is not defined in any dictionary as humor.

So with these core beliefs in place, I ask them clarifying, and sometimes probing, questions. I politely offer ideas, suggestions, and feedback (see *Brain Connection 5-a*), but I am careful not to remove the pen from the hand that owns the writing. There is no room in my writing classroom for right and wrong responses, only reflection questions and comments to be weighed against original ideas.

I once read a teacher's defense of "the red pen." She argued that her red marks showed her passion for writing, and that she used red—the Valentine's Day

3 Core Beliefs

1. Every student is good at some type of writing.

2. Practice patience when learners just don't seem to "get it."

3. Avoid sarcasm which robs students of the trust they need to have with teachers.

color—because she loved her students. I agree with her sentiments 100 percent: We need to help our learners appreciate that constructive criticism is a sign of caring and that writing is most satisfying when the reader understands what we're saying—the way we mean it. However, some of the most well read and respected pieces of literature break the rules we teachers so often work to enforce. Let's keep in mind that even the rules of literature and grammar change and evolve with time. Our students will be these change-makers.

> As brain-compatible writing teachers, we need to help learners relinquish first-draft ideas without relinquishing their self-esteem.

Will driving learners to perform the demanding task of revision cause too much stress? Yes... and no. Driving students to achieve mastery, or the desire to, is an example of good stress (see *Brain Connection 5-b*); that is, *if* you've implemented Principle #1 and have established a safe and caring environment. The learning activity on page 154 encourages the process of constructive criticism and the collegial feedback without threatening or judging the writer's own work/process:

Brain Connection 5-a
Balanced Feedback Best

Research findings suggest that the spoken word and verbal feedback during and after a learning task are key elements in the error-correction process (Rogers 1998). However, feedback given continuously and concurrently during learning can actually impede training, a recent study reports (Schmidt 1997). In the Schmidt experiment, subjects that received continuous kinetic feedback about errors during discreet movement learning acquired their skills at a slower rate than those who did not receive continuous concurrent feedback.

 ## Classroom Applications

From these studies, we've gained a few important teaching and learning insights:

It's smart to incorporate inherent forms of feedback such as self-check lists, quizzes, and peer-review instruments. There is value in verbal feedback or talking about a learning process. Intervening too soon or too often in the learning process can undermine information acquisition and retention. Monitoring student progress through direct teacher assistance is one of the most important roles a teacher has. Tell students what they're doing well and ask provocative questions to stimulate further learning. Post checklists, learning goals, and recognition charts on the walls. Learners need ways to know if they're on track!

*For full citations, see "References" in Appendix.

Learning Activity:
Setting the Stage for Constructive Feedback

Locate a weak writing sample, such as the one following and use it to teach appropriate conferencing/feedback techniques.

-Sample Draft-

Autumn

The trees' look nice they are pretty. I like to walk threw the leaves, sometimes its windy. Then my friends and me go roller-blading. Roller-blading is cool my friends think their better than me no way! I'm the best. The other day I jumped over a gigantic ramp...

Place a copy of the writing sample on your overhead or hand out copies. Ask for a volunteer—with a thick skin—to pretend the piece is his or hers. Direct the learner to read the piece aloud and ask you: "Will you be my conference partner?" Now the fun begins. Have the volunteer ask you to answer the following questions:

1. *What's the strongest part in my work?*
2. *What's the weakest part in my work?*
3. *Does my work have a clear purpose and direction?*
4. *Do you have any questions about it?*
5. *Do you have any suggestions for it?*

For the first round, be unmerciful: "There is no strong part. All of it! NO! Why'd you write it? Dump it."

After you are done with your verbal lashing, ask the class: "How'd I do? Was I an effective conferencing partner?" Trust me. Kids know. They will most assuredly let you know you were "so mean."

The second go-round, be really sticky-sweet as you respond to the questions. "All of it. There is none.

Everything's fine. No. Not a thing... just write it a second time so the teacher sees a first draft." Once again ask the class to comment, and once again they will let you know you were "too nice" and you were "lying."

Ask a more discerning student what you should have said and how you should have said it. What follows, of course, are responses that demonstrate polite and constructive feedback—responses that produce effective revision suggestions for a writer to consider.

Examples of Constructive Feedback

◆ "Walking through the leaves" creates a pleasurable visual image of autumn. I wanted to hear more about that. Is there more you could share with the reader about this experience? Remember the 5-Ws (Who, What, When, Where, Why). The more details you can provide, the more the reader will feel like they're walking through the leaves with you.

◆ When the mood shifts suddenly from walking through the leaves on a windy day to roller-blading, I feel ripped off. I want to know more about "Autumn" and what that means to you. Is there more you might tell the reader about your walk in the leaves?

◆ Although the words "threw" and "through" are pronounced the same, they have different meanings. Let's define them and see which one fits this context.

◆ When you read your writing out loud, are there places where a pause is natural? What punctuation marks tell the reader it's time to pause. Do you have them in place? Let's read the piece together and see.

◆ Did you proofread your work when you were done writing it? Were there words that you weren't sure how to spell. Let's review your piece and use the dictionary to help us correct words that may not be spelled how they sound.

◆ Let's break down the sentence that reads "Then my friends and me go roller-blading." Do you sense that a grammar rule has been broken here? What might that rule be and how can we check ourselves to ensure the sentence is written correctly?

The Homework Question

When it comes to the question of whether homework is beneficial to learning, a whole set of other questions surfaces. What is the primary purpose of the homework? How will success be measured? Is the assignment aligned with the identified learning goals? At what stage of the learning curve are students? How motivated are they to learn? Can we ensure students are practicing good technique at home? What support mechanisms are in place to assist students should they need help in the process? And, what if learners try really hard, but get all the wrong answers? What kind of damage might this cause our fledgling writers?

Unfortunately, many teachers don't consider these critical questions when preparing homework assignments. Instead, we send them home with yet another workbook assignment. You know the kind—they read more like exercises in drudgery than opportunities for creative self-expression. Conjugate these verbs; define these terms; write a report on the life of Abraham Lincoln. We give learners less than a day to complete the work and then we expect them to *want* to "learn" more after completing the chore. On top of this, we penalize students if they don't accomplish the task, despite the fact that not all learners have the same support at home. Textbook assignments may assuage parents who insist on homework, but they do little to promote an interest in real writing. Do we want to promote rote responses, copying, confusion, and boredom? Teaching and learning loses much of its luster when we force students to do things their brains don't enjoy or aren't ready for.

Consider this: Would a good soccer coach send the team home to practice goal-keeping regardless of a player's skill level or position on the team? Would a golf coach have a student practice tennis swings? Would a ski instructor send kids home to write a report about skiing?

As writing coaches, we need to plan homework assignments with great care and thought. The tendency, for example, to give peripheral assignments to writing (i.e., grammar rules & spelling exercises) are apt to turn young learners off, rather than on, to the pure act of unrestrained self-expression. This is especially true when writing "rules" are overemphasized or presented prematurely. If, on the other hand, the writer is ready—they have reached the stage of development in which grammar rules are becoming truly meaningful—a related homework assignment may be very productive. Bottom line: If you're going to assign homework, ask the critical questions that ensure your assignments are aligned with how the brain actually learns. In other words, consider and accommodate for developmental appropriateness, meaningfulness, safety, feedback, attention, downtime, and environment.

Clearly, we can reduce undesirable homework consequences by devising thoughtful assignments that emphasize critical thinking, self expression, and pure writing practice—like the homework assignments emphasized throughout *Write Brain Write*.

Homework activities that are appealing to the student can foster authentic learning. However, only when learners demonstrate competency in "real time" (not on grades based on what they fail to do or what's done at home) can authentic assessment be ensured. And nowhere is this truer than in the writing classroom.

To ensure authentic assessment we must first plan formative writing activities that promote ongoing, real-time writing, and second, implement tools like rubrics that encourage students to assess their own progress (see Chapter 6 and Appendix). Students gain a stronger understanding of what good work looks and sounds like when they discover and produce such work in their classroom work environment.

In the final analysis, homework may be a valid formative assessment instrument if assigned and graded from the "practice-makes-perfect" philosophic base, not the "all-or-nothing, check mark or goose egg" base of yesteryear. Personally, I think it's unfair to ask children to do what the majority of adults don't do—work after work. Most adults indulge in a little relaxation after a hard day's work. I believe young writers are entitled to the same down time, especially if we create rigorous, demanding environments that encourage hard work and produce clear evidence that our classrooms are workplaces of learning.

Welcome to Cheats 'R' Us Dot Com

Here's another reason to think about homework's place in the new millennium. Surf the net for homework and you will find sites like the one mentioned above as well as Cool Cheats, Homework Cheats and Cheater.Com. After typing in "homework cheats" on one search engine, I was asked: "Are you looking for Cheats, Cheat Homework Test Exam, Ways to Cheat on your Homework, Homework Cheat Papers, or Cheat on Homework?" Yikes!

What About Standardized Tests?

When it comes to the complicated question of standardized testing, there is no right or wrong answer, only the reality of the education business. The threat of national writing assessment tests has swept the nation. The stakes are high and getting higher; some states threaten to dangle the carrot of graduation from the test paper's perforations.

Why aren't our nation's students showing higher proficiency scores on these writing tests? Brains require safety, first and foremost. The unfamiliar testing instruments themselves may be a large part of the problem! Such writing tests are not only alien to how students really write, they are alien to many teachers. Unfamiliar and suspect, is it any wonder students perform less well than expected on standardized tests?

The National Assessment Governing Board (NAGB) oversees the National Assessment for Educational Progress (NAEP), the "Nation's Report Card" people who become important each time their score results hit the papers. NAEP is actually our ally, having discovered that 89 percent of the variance of its national testing scores is explained by four variables: (1) the number of parents living in the home; (2) the parents' education level; (3) the type of community; and (4) a state's poverty rate (Ramirez 1999). How interesting that the variables associated with these test score results support the brain's need for a safe, nurturing environment.

Prospects for success need not remain so bleak however. Brains do respond independent of safety and novelty. In fact, a little stress can actually move learners in a positive direction (see *Brain Connection 5-b*). This is where the writing teacher's acumen comes into play. We need to excite kids to feel "good" stress—the kind that pumps them up to "win" the testing game. We know that teachers set the tone in classrooms. We can role-model a positive, constructive attitude by minimizing our negativity about administering standardized tests and rather behaving like coaches, pumping up the team for the "the big game." As we express confidence in our students throughout the year and groom them for success during rehearsal time (see *Brain Connection 5-c*), we increase their success when the testing show, alas, must go on.

Brain Connection 5-b
The Neurobiology of Stress

Research reveals that psychological stress is not inherently bad. In fact, when we are under-aroused, we usually lack the stimulation to perform optimally and boredom sets in. Conversely, a chronically high level of stress damages brain cells, impacting both learning ability and physical health over time (Borella, et al. 1999; Clement & Chapouthier 1998; Sheline, et al. 1999). Moderate stress—the kind produced by reasonable assignment deadlines, accountability expectations, and healthy competition—is just what the brain needs for optimal learning.

While we know that chronic forms of stress can impact memory and attention, as well as destroy the immune system's "killer cells" which help the body fight off disease and infection, studies examining test anxiety shed further light on what constitutes destructive stress.

Sephton (1996) found in a study of 36 college undergraduates with high levels of stress that damage to subjects' immune system "killer cells" increased 52 percent during performance of a verbal arithmetic task. The researchers also noted increased levels of the stress-sensitive hormone cortisol in subjects, which in elevated amounts damages the hippocampus, a critical part of the brain involved in learning and memory formation. The Borella team (1999) reported similar results in a study involving 39 military cadets during academic examinations, and Cohen (1999) found a clear relationship between psychological stress and increased risk of infection by respiratory virus, particularly the common cold.

Brain Connection 5-b continued...

On the positive side, studies by Kellogg and colleagues (1999) and Hardy and Parfitt (1991) reveal that moderate stress levels can have a motivating effect in the school environment. The Kellogg team found that moderate stress induced by a timed arithmetic performance test actually motivated both anxious and non-anxious students to better apply previously learned principles. And in a study whereby experienced collegiate basketball players were asked to shoot baskets under varying levels of cognitive stress, Hardy and Parfitt found that players operating under moderately high levels of pressure significantly outperformed those acting under low pressure.

The key to thriving under stress and making stressors work for, rather than against, us is an intense feeling of self-confidence to cope with the task at hand, combined with a healthy dose of self-esteem, concludes a 1999 study led by Israeli psychologist Yoram Bar-Tal. When these keys are in place, positive pressure can enhance decision-making, information processing, and new learning applications.

When we perceive a situation as challenging, but non-threatening, the proper stage is set in our brain for alterations in neural networks to occur, thus aiding our ability to think, plan, and remember. To help us do this, our brain releases such cognitive-enhancing neurotransmitters as acetylcholine, interferon, and interleukins, while maintaining a moderate level of cortisol and adrenaline. This balance allows learners to react enthusiastically and logically to challenges.

*For full citations, see "References" in Appendix.

 Classroom Applications

To mediate anxiety caused, for example, by high-stakes standardized tests, we must better prepare students. Encourage them to learn from mistakes, rather than shy away from them. Have them notice how extreme stress impacts their body and mind. Incorporate pre-tests, writing exercises, and practice reviews prior to the exam. See to it that learners demonstrate a competence at basic or fundamental levels before advancing to the next level. Maintain challenging, but realistic standards and hold learners accountable. Introduce a healthy dose of peer competition and, when appropriate, use cooperative teams for accomplishing tasks. Praise and encourage anxious learners, especially when stress is handled in a positive manner. If teachers view themselves as coaches, gearing their players up for the big "test" game, students will learn how to manage stress—to use it as a motivation to prepare and succeed.

One way to prepare learners for taking standardized tests is to do mock tests in class which reflect the format of the real thing. For example, get students used to the pattern and procedure of answering questions. Will they be expected to circle the correct answer on the test itself or to pencil in a corresponding bubble on a separate answer sheet? What should they do if they don't know the answer? How much time should they spend on a question? Have them practice answering questions, penciling in the bubbles, erasing answers, and deciding what to do with a question when they don't know the answer. Such practice reduces the mental stress that can occur under pressure.

*For full citations, see "References" in Appendix.

Brain Connection 5-c
The Power of Prep-tests

Students who take practice exams, pre-tests, or structured preparation courses stand to significantly increase their actual test scores, suggests recent research (Chan 1998; Miller 1996). Positive results are even more significant when students are motivated to take such practice tests, suggests Chan (ibid.).

Practice, especially under voluntary and motivated circumstances, sets the brain up for meaningful learning by converting information from short- to long-term memory. Practice also lessens the brain's fear or anxiety response to the unknown (located in the amygdala) and strengthens the neural connections that are formed while learning and receiving feedback.

A positive attitude is known to virtually alter the chemistry of the brain, fostering the production of dopamine—a "feel-good" neurotransmitter—which propels optimism and noradrenaline, which provides physical energy to act upon motivations. And ultimately attitude influences the activation of the frontal lobes, which are responsible for long-term planning and judgment.

In a study of 38 undergraduates participating in an intensive, structured self-paced Graduate Record Examination (GRE) preparatory course over 7 weeks (involving 66-140 hours of study), Jan Miller reported significant improvements between pre- and post-test verbal, quantitative, and combined scores. In one series, the mean combined scores improved 96 points, increasing from 842 (pre-test) to 938 (post-test). In another series, the mean improved 186 points, increasing from 888 to 1074. Miller adds, participants were basically motivated and were offered attendance and participation incentives.

Brain Connection 5-c continued...

Chan also reported significant pre-test and post-test improvements involving 197 undergraduates participating in a cognitive ability evaluation. And Briton and Virean (1999) noted in a study of 381 undergraduates involved in a supplemental instruction program that post-test results improved when students combined classroom practice with peer instruction.

 Classroom Applications

Remember pre-tests are most effective when learners are motivated. Thus, combine low-stakes pre-testing with meaningful peer interaction, practice, and incremental feedback for best results. This research emphasizes the importance of being a pro-active teacher who prepares learners before high-stakes tests by implementing interesting and purposeful rehearsal strategies. Too often, teachers implement pre-testing activities begrudgingly or marginally, modeling for their students the worse possible attitude for success.

Give learners meaningful multiple-choice quizzes throughout the year that replicate the answer format (e.g., lettered bubble-sheet grid in the right column of each test page) used in the standardized test. This practice gives learners a familiarity with the procedure and with the fine motor skills that "bubbling" requires.

*For full citations, see "References" in Appendix.

Real-Life Application:
The "Clue" to Exact Writing

In teaching the art of forming precise sentences, I like to incorporate the novelty and intrigue of mystery writing. I've found that the old board game Clue (with a twist) engages learners and *shows* students the value of exact writing.

The game involves drafting the opening paragraphs of a mystery. Students readily agree that if writers fail to grab the reader's attention at the very beginning, it is unlikely that the story will be read all the way through. The goal then becomes the exploration of the mystery writer's craft—learning what it means to "hook" the reader and keep them hooked with exact writing.

Learning Objective:
Students will learn how to identify and revise vague or imprecise language while drafting the beginning of a mystery.

Method/Plan:
◆ This learning activity is well-suited for teacher-facilitated whole-group instruction. Students' desks can be arranged in a configuration of learning pairs, giving them the option to work alone or together. Facilitate teacher-to-student dialogue and team conferencing as the game plays out.

◆ Prepare transparencies or handouts (cover Teacher-Tips before copying) and distribute.

◆ Have students write their responses directly on pre-produced activity sheets or as notes on paper in response to your overhead presentation.

From Vague to Exact Writing

<u>Writing Goal:</u> Today we'll learn how to improve our writing skills by using clear and precise language!

<u>Example 1: Vague and Boring:</u>
Someone disappeared.

<u>Better:</u> One night someone disappeared.

<u>Exact and Exciting:</u> One dark and stormy night when the wind howled and shutters slammed against their window frames, the well-loved professor disappeared.

<u>Example 2: Vague and Boring:</u>
✏ Someone heard something.

<u>Exact (Who?):</u>
✏ The frightened child
✏ The unsuspecting professor

<u>Exact (What?)</u>
✏ A faint whistle
✏ Sirens
✏ Glass shatter

<u>Revision Examples:</u>
The frightened child screamed when she heard the glass shatter.

"What could that be," the professor pondered as he bent his ear towards a faint whistle that seemed to be coming from high atop a massive old oak tree.

<u>Your Turn to Practice:</u> Revise the following vague sentence examples so that they become exact and exciting.

<u>Example 1: Vague and Boring:</u> Someone disappeared.

Better:

_____

_____

_____

Exact and Exciting:

_____

_____

_____

<u>Example 2: Vague and Boring:</u> Someone heard something.

Better:

_____

_____

_____

Exact and Exciting:

_____

_____

_____

Teacher Tip:

Read the goal and sample sentence aloud (or have a student do it). Provide the necessary time to discuss and complete the task. Encourage students to share their responses. Write several sample responses on the board, focusing on the power of exact words and precise phrases. Emphasize how the revision process can transform a piece of writing from good to great!

Get Down...time!

After completing the above activity, provide some purposeful down time by playing a very modified version of Clue. In the game atmosphere, the importance of exact language is reinforced without conscious effort on the student's part.

Get a "Clue"

Let's examine the following vague opening sentence to our mystery and revise it with exact and exciting language that hooks readers into wanting to read more:

<u>Vague:</u>
A person in a room killed someone with something.

How can we make this opening sentence more exact and exciting?

Student Responses:

_____

_____

_____

_____

_____

_____

_____

_____

_____

_____

Teacher Tip:
After brainstorming responses to the question above, ask learners to choose their own version of the mystery based on the characters and situations represented by the clue cards represented in Reproducible 5:3.

At this point some students invariably blurt out their familiarity with the sentence, since it reflects the gist of the Clue Game. Seize this opportunity to illustrate how vague and boring the game would be if we did not know the exact information about who, where, what, etc. By playing a micro-mini version of Clue, we celebrate Brain-Compatible Principle III: We feed the brains' love of novelty with an engaging appetizer that ultimately leads to the satisfying main course.

Choose Your Clue Cards

Vague: A person...

Exact: COLONEL MUSTARD   MR. GREEN
           MISS SCARLETT   MRS. PEACOCK
           PROFESSOR PLUM

Vague: ... in a room...

Exact: LIBRARY   HALL
           KITCHEN   DINING ROOM
           BILLIARD ROOM

Vague: ... killed someone... (Choose someone different than murderer!)

Exact: COLONEL MUSTARD   MR. GREEN
           MISS SCARLETT   MRS. PEACOCK
           PROFESSOR PLUM

Vague: ... with something!

Exact: LEAD PIPE   ROPE
           KNIFE   WRENCH
           CANDLESTICK   REVOLVER

Create Your Own Story

What person?_____

Where?_____

Killed whom?_____

With what? _____

Teacher Tip:

Before starting, create your own game cards depicting the above characters and situations. You may wish to incorporate this task into an art lesson. I confess, I use the real cards from a Clue game I bought years ago at a yard sale.

After choosing their own responses (i.e., who, what, when, where) to transform the above vague sentence into an exciting and exact opening sentence, have four students draw one card from each pile. Slip the selected cards to be revealed at the end of class into an envelope marked "Confidential." Students then compare their own story selections with the "confidential" one: Did anyone solve the mystery? Playing mystery music in the background adds a nice touch during this activity.

The Challenge

✏ Write the opening paragraph of a mystery.

✏ Use precise and exact language.
Leave the reader desperate to know what happens next!

✏ Don't reveal or explain the disappearance in your first paragraph.

✏ Experiment with your words! Is there a better way to phrase what you wish to say?

Vague:
I was scared when I went to the haunted house.

Better:
As I walked through the haunted house, a chill surged down my spine.

Exact:
A chill surged down my spine as I tiptoed down the long dark hall of the mansion said to be haunted.

....

Vague:
I felt like shouting, but I was too scared to say a word.

Better:
"I want to go home... Help me!" I felt like shouting, but the words wouldn't come.

Exact:
"I want to go home! Help me!" I felt like shouting, but the words froze deep in my throat.

Try it yourself:
As you review your drafts, circle potentially vague and boring words/phrases (like the examples below) for later revision:

✏ There was...
✏ One day...
✏ Once...
✏ It sounded, tasted, smelled, felt, or looked like...
✏ Go/Went   Come/Came   See/Saw
✏ I saw the full moon.
✏ I heard a noise.
✏ I felt sick.
✏ I smelled something strange.

Student Mystery Samples

Jocelyn, Age 12

I hid under my covers listening to the rain
pound on the roof as if it were trying to get in.
Thunder screamed at me as loud as it could. It
shot down and set a nearby tree on fire. The
lights flickered and for a moment everything
grew silent and I could hear something down-
stairs. The rain and thunder continued. The
storm scared me because I was a child. I knew
people got murdered during storms. I didn't
want to get murdered. Wait, I thought. Am I asleep? Is this just a
nightmare? Oh please be a nightmare. Please let me wake up. I want it
to be morning.

Dan, Age 13

The wind howled against the hearse as it lurched toward the foggy
graveyard. The funeral procession had moved like a lazy caterpillar
on a warm summer's day. We finally reached the site in three hours.
While the dark but holy figure read the blessings, a shrill ear-pierc-
ing cry came from within the coffin. It was gone as quickly as it had
come. Only two words came to my mind: "Buried alive!"

Nash, Age 13

Her eyes glazed over with fear, almost to the point where she could
no longer see the window, or what was outside it. A blurred image of
a hand scratched the window. Once, twice, three times. Her heart
fluttered and her breath froze in her throat. She clenched her
sweaty palms together and rubbed her eyes, but when she looked
again nothing was there. She sighed, sure she had just imagined it,
but then she heard it again. Although this time it was not at the window, but at her bedroom door. The knob turned slowly, and with each
agonizing turn she felt her fate coming nearer. The door flung open,
hitting the wall with a boom. She opened her mouth to scream, but
before she could get a sound out, it was over.

Not bad for seventh graders!!!

Playing the Game of Exact Language

If they wish to, please let students continue their mysteries. Though the genre of mystery writing itself may not be addressed in most curricula guides, fictional narration usually is. Give learners the choice of writing in the genre that appeals to their natural curiosity and interests. Everyone likes options. Suggest fables, folktales, adventure, sci-fi, or the completion of their mystery.

The following guidelines will help students work independently while writing their mysteries. Perhaps they will choose to share their stories on "Author's Day" (see Chapter 6). For younger students, writing a scene is more realistic than writing an entire story. Pre-high-schoolers are frequently unable to sustain the precision of language and the complexity of plot required for the completion of a mystery. Of course, you are the best judge of your students. If you invite them to experiment with writing a complete mystery, remind them to maintain effective word choice and sentence fluency throughout the story, while staying mindful of the conceptual and organizational requirements of a complete work of fiction.

Once your students demonstrate their ability to write with precision, help them encode their acquired writing skills by inviting them to bring in examples of writing work from other classes. Challenge them to identify and improve weak or imprecise language in all of their varied assignments. What good is writing with precision in a creative writing class, if students don't see how precision relates to every type of writing?

Collaborate with colleagues. Request examples of social studies and science essays that fail to address prompts or to demonstrate understanding of a topic because of imprecise or ambiguous language.

By helping kids learn the "game" of exact language in and out of one content area, we help them hardwire their understanding of this essential lifelong skill across disciplines. Students who learn the art of articulation now will excel tomorrow in our fast-paced world where extreme communication is the name of the game.

 In Review

1. What brain-compatible principles do you incorporate to ensure that students' experience of the revision process is threat-free and constructive?

2. Do you regularly assign homework? If so, how do the assignments align with the critical questions outlined in this chapter?

3. How do you prepare learners for the "big test game"? What brain-compatible principles do you apply in the process?

*R*ight On, Write On

More to Writing than Good Spelling: Authentic Assessment Systems

As brain-compatible writing teachers, we must insist on authentic and comprehensive assessment systems. Too many teachers still evaluate students' abilities based exclusively on convention, mechanics, or test scores. How sad for intrapersonal, musical children whose voice and wit and sensitivity are lost on teachers who don't include, for example, writers' voice, descriptive word choice, or dramatic sentence fluency in their evaluation process.

Brain-compatible teachers diversify their techniques so that all learners' strengths and weaknesses are viewed in a comprehensive manner. Many advocate student portfolios as a holistic approach for archiving assignments and documenting progress. Portfolios also provide a tidy way for students to share their work during open houses or on parent night. In addition, they give students a historical base from which to realize their own progress over the course of the term. And they provide an orderly mechanism for teachers to evaluate students on an ongoing basis.

> Self-evaluation instruments, as one component of a comprehensive assessment portfolio, keep learners in the driver's seat—an important aspect of a well-rounded brain-friendly assessment system.

A variety of assessment measures ought to be included within the portfolio file—for example, standardized tests, in-class quizzes, homework assignments, partner assessments, self-assessments, and teacher-facilitated evaluation rubrics. Standardized evaluation measures are important because they help ensure that children are scored uniformly. Standardized charts (also called "rubrics") give all learners a fair chance, including those who tend to be scored harshly due to peripheral issues like behavior challenges, language barriers, or spelling/grammar weaknesses. Self-evaluation instruments are also integral to the process because they put the onus of responsibility back on the learner. In other words, they keep the learner in the "driver's seat"—an important component of a well-rounded and brain-friendly assessment system.

Brain Connection 6-a
The Brain's Error Correction Process

Most people probably never wonder what occurs in their brain when they make a mistake; scientists, however, have diligently pursued the question. Recent studies suggest that two executive systems in the brain's frontal region, the frontal eye field and the cingulate cortex, react when we make a mistake, thereby helping us to correct it (Carter, et al. 1998; McDonald, et al. 2000; Stuphorn, et al. 2000).

The Carter team found that the anterior cingulate cortex, located on the medial surface of the frontal lobe, contributes to cognitive performance by detecting errors. More specifically, this region detects conditions under which errors are likely to occur rather than errors themselves. A later study by the MacDonald team (Carter served as a co-author), found that the anterior cingulate cortex was especially adept at detecting and responding to incongruent stimuli or data during mental processing.

Solving difficult, novel, or complex tasks, overcoming habitual responses, and correcting errors all require a high degree of cognitive control. Acting as the brain's "mistake filters," the frontal eye field and anterior cingulate cortex, it appears, critically impact our thoughts, actions, and errors.

In a study examining the frontal eye field, a brain area that exercises direct control over eye movements, the Stuphorn team suggests this region regulates its own activity as it makes decisions, corrects errors, and overrides habitual responses. The critical point here is that when we can actually see the errors we make, we learn to correct them more quickly.

 **Classroom Applications**

Rather than simply pointing out mistakes, help learners to identify themselves where and how their logic became faulty. Remember, when we can see our mistakes, the frontal eye field—which houses our error-correction and overriding faculties—is activated. This is partly why self-assessment rubrics are so powerful as learning devices. Once learners have identified their writing weaknesses, guide them through the correct steps, thus, reinforcing accurate methods. Create a learning environment that helps students feel comfortable and safe and smart despite mistakes. Reassure students that mistakes are how we learn. Allow sufficient "down time" for reflection and consolidation of new learning subsequent to feedback sessions.

*For full citations, see "References" in Appendix.

The Rubric Bandwagon

Evaluation rubrics have emerged lately as the "new" trend in education. Although myriad states are now jumping on the rubric "bandwagon," many teachers have used criteria assessment instruments (i.e., "rubrics") for years. Rubrics provide a standardization of the evaluation process based on very specific criteria (e.g., every "t" is crossed and "i" dotted) and benchmarks (i.e., superior to or below grade-level standard). Many writing teachers, myself included, rely heavily on rubrics as part of our total evaluation process. Although no system is completely objective, rubrics come close.

Many writing teachers see district- and state-imposed writing rubric systems as yet another outside interference. Yes, the challenge is formidable. Some districts require participation in intensive training workshops, while others virtually toss volumes of information at schools, expecting teachers to decipher and implement the new program independently. Our brains tend to balk at such coercion and indifference. Our sense of anger and frustration is tremendous when we don't understand or necessarily agree with a mandated "intervention." On the other hand, once we understand the value of rubrics and how they promote meaningful learning experiences, we can benefit from the support offered at the higher levels.

Consistent and uniform scoring systems work for everyone in every state. I was fortunate enough to begin my teaching career in a district where the language-arts program was coordinated by the visionary Edie Wagner. Edie conveyed the educational importance of rubric charts to her teachers long before other districts began advocating their use. I followed her lead and after 16 years of teaching, I can wholeheartedly say her insight has proven right. You'll be amazed at how quickly your students learn to rely on rubrics, and how much they complement your evaluation process. Whether or not your district or state advocates rubrics, read on. This flexible evaluation technique may be the single most effective way to empower students with a real understanding of what proficient writing looks like.

Rubrics as Personal Roadmaps

What better way to get students engaged in their own learning than to have them self-evaluate their work? But how do we prepare the way for this? Without a well-developed roadmap, students can't possibly reach the intended destination. Rubrics offer a brain-compatible tool for guiding learners through the self-assessment process, ultimately helping them to become critical thinkers, realistic self-assessors, and proficient writers.

Think about it: Isn't it easier to reach an unfamiliar destination when we have a good map and clear directions? And, doesn't it make good brain sense to have students and teachers "on the same page" when it comes to learning standards? Rubrics provide a precise definition of each expected learning skill and are followed by clear objectives and measurable criteria for defining an individual's level of mastery in constructive terms. Rubrics ensure a smooth path to proficiency, reducing roadblocks such as fuzzy expectations, fluctuating objectives, and/or non-existent standards along the way. The best rubrics are flexible mechanisms that are easily adapted for self-assessment, group assessment, peer assessment, or instructor assessment purposes. You will be introduced to examples of each later in this chapter.

Everyone benefits from rubrics, but kids especially like the opportunity rubrics provide to "play teacher"-to score their own work and that of their peers. The National Training Laboratories cites that students retain 70 percent of what they learn when they practice as they learn and 90 percent of what they learn when they *teach others* (see Appendix E: *The Learning Pyramid*). With rubrics, learners teach each other by their very conversations. Not only do they benefit from being exposed to the language and criteria of rubrics, they profit from learning how to self-administer feedback through each stage of the writing process. Isn't it easier to reach instructional goals when we know precisely what they are? Rubrics provide a built-in feedback mechanism that enables us to individualize our own instruction!

I always ask students to self-assess their assignments before turning in a final copy. I recommend they use both the Self-Assessment Rubric (Reprographic 6:1), which gives them an opportunity to score their own work, and the Writing Rubric Chart (Appendix F), which asks them to circle the appropriate descriptors for each skill-set. Sometimes I ask learners to justify their responses, which helps me determine whether they are actively using the charts or merely going through the motions.

The National Training Laboratories cites that students retain 70% of what they learn when they practice as they learn and 90% of what they learn when they <u>teach others</u>. With rubrics, learners teach each other by their very conversations.

Then with their completed evaluations attached to their papers, I use a yellow highlighter to *assess their self-assessments*. Where a descriptor is circled that I agree with, I concur by highlighting over it. This procedure reveals two things: whether students are proficient in each of the writing trait categories, and whether they know they are proficient.

The self-assessment process not only results in less work for me because students discover their own errors and weaknesses, it is good for learning. When students discover their own errors, the research suggests, they are more likely to learn from them (see Brain Connection 6-a).

Rubrics Rule

Take a look at the sample rubric charts included in this chapter and compare them with the evaluation measures your school or state requires. Discuss the differences between them; share them with colleagues and students; then revise them to suit your needs. I like to vary the paper color between types of rubrics and assignments so that they're easy to identify in students' portfolios/folders. And, for the sake of simplicity, I also sometimes synthesize the five core writing skill sets (Idea, Content, Organization, Word Choice, Sentence Fluency, and Voice) into the umbrella term "content." I tell students that *content* is *what* they write while *mechanics* is *how* they write it.

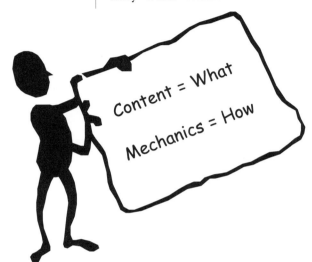

Content can be evaluated (at least partly) at the draft or brainstorm stage (i.e., effectiveness of idea, organization, etc.) but the *mechanics* of a piece cannot be evaluated until it is actually written.

Introduce the skill sets included in the rubric chart one trait at a time. The skills associated with *mechanics* are usually a good place to start because they tend to be pretty concrete and most learners are accustomed to having spelling and grammatical errors pointed out to them. Follow with the more abstract concepts associated with *content*. Voice can be challenging to explain, so you may want to focus on it last.

Note:
Additional reproducible rubric charts to assess writing, reading, group work, oral presentations, and debate are included in Appendix F.

Student Self-Assessment Rubric

Writing Skill-Sets		
Idea	Word Choice	Voice
Organization	Sentence Fluency	Mechanics

Author's Name:_____Date:_____

Title of Work:_____Type of Work:_____

Refer to your Writing Skills Training Manual for descriptions of the following skills/traits.

CONTENT
Idea/Concept: I give myself a_____ because...
Organization: I give myself a_____ because...
Word Choice: I give myself a_____ because...
Sentence Fluency: I give myself a_____ because...
Voice/Style: I give myself a_____ because...

MECHANICS
Conventions: I give myself a_____ because...

6	5	4	3	2	1
outstanding		meets standard		needs revision	

COMMENTS
What improvements might I make as your teacher to help you as a writer or our class in general?_____
_____

Remember: Writers must be their own worst critics. Write on!

Teacher Tip:
Before asking students to administer the Self-Assessment Rubric, use student examples to illustrate each of the above listed writing skill-sets.

Instructor-Assessment Rubric

Author's Name:_____Date:_____

CONTENT

Idea/Concept: Your writing exhibits an understanding of this skill.
       Yes   Not Yet   Partly
Comment:_____

Organization: Your writing exhibits an understanding of this skill.
       Yes   Not Yet   Partly
Comment:_____

Word Choice: Your writing exhibits an understanding of this skill.
       Yes   Not Yet   Partly
Comment:_____

Sentence Fluency: Your writing exhibits an understanding of this skill.
       Yes   Not Yet   Partly
Comment:_____

Voice/Style: Your writing exhibits an understanding of this skill.
       Yes   Not Yet   Partly
Comment:_____

MECHANICS

Conventions: Your writing exhibits an understanding of the skills associated with spelling and grammar.
       Yes   Not Yet   Partly
Comment:_____

COMMENTS

My recommendation for future growth is:_____
_____
_____
_____

Peer-Assessment Rubric

Assessor's Name:_____

Date:_____

Author's Name:_____

Assignment:_____

CONTENT

Read your partner's work and evaluate it using the checklist below. Next to each criteria, write Yes, No, or Needs Improvement.

1. The content addresses the prompt/assignment?_____

2. It is clearly organized?_____

3. Supporting material is provided?_____

4. Language is clear and concise?_____

5. A satisfying conclusion is provided? _____

Based on the above results, how would you score the content?

6	5	4	3	2	1
outstanding		meets standard		needs revision	

-continued-

MECHANICS

1. Re-read the work carefully. Underline words you are certain are misspelled or grammatically incorrect.

2. Underline words/phrases that are confusing or awkward.

Based on your above answers, how would you score the mechanics of this paper?

6	5	4	3	2	1
outstanding		meets standard		needs revision	

COMPLIMENTS/COMMENTS

Describe for your writing partner how you arrived at your assessment score. What was done well and/or what may need improvement?_____

_____

_____

_____

_____

After sharing this worksheet with your conference partner, ask him/her to circle a response to the following two questions.

I agree with my partner's assessment.   Yes   No

I plan on revising my work to improve it.   Yes   No

Paper's Author: _____

Author's Signature: _____

End-of-Term Self-Evaluation Rubric

Students Name:_____Date:_____

Choose 4 out of the 7 following statements to answer in complete sentences. Your answers may reflect any part of your life, not just your experiences in this class.

1. The high point of this term was...

_____

_____

2. The low point of this term was...

_____

_____

3. My term would have been better if...

_____

_____

4. This class would be better if...

_____

_____

5. School would be better if...

_____

_____

6. Something about my behavior that I like most is...

_____

_____

7. Something about my behavior that I want to work on is...

_____

_____

Vocabulary: A Matter of Relevance

How can we be certain that students know the meaning of the terms used in their rubrics (i.e., fluency, relevant, vague, appropriate)? By teaching them. Self-assessment rubrics provide the perfect springboard for creating a vocabulary workshop that is completely "relevant" to students. I introduce the terms early in the year through a fun activity that eventually leads students to the computer lab where they create colorful "Writing Skills Training Manuals" that help them "learn the lingo." Challenge students to work together, to examine, discuss, and define the very specific objectives outlined in their Training Manuals. The following is a sample of one student's explanation of the vocabulary word "appropriate" as listed in his Training Manual:

Appropriate - *suitable or compatible*
A champagne toast was very appropriate for the Y2K celebration.

 Brain Connection 6-b
The Importance of Applying New Learning

Verbally or physically repeating newly learned material (sometimes referred to as "drill & practice") is a low-cognitive demand process that helps the brain store information in short-term memory. However, to make it stick in long-term memory, the learner must apply the new material in various performance situations, suggests research by Goodwin and colleagues (1998). And when practical applications of a newly learned skill are followed by immediate and frequent feedback, memory is further enhanced, the researchers add (ibid).

Brain Connection 6-b continued...

In a study on memory involving 80 undergraduate students, the Goodwin team found that recall and retention was significantly improved when students applied their new knowledge and skills within two hours of learning, and when the tasks were carried out in varied performance situations followed by regular feedback.

While the physical and verbal repetitiveness of drill and practice demands little cognitive effort, gaining understanding of how a skill relates to practical, everyday situations requires greater cognitive effort and, therefore, supports long-term memory storage and recall.

 ## Classroom Applications

Drill and practice by itself can reinforce certain things like basic math, reading, and writing skills. However, getting students to think about why they are learning these skills and how the new knowledge relates to the "bigger picture" is essential. For example, in teaching the rules of grammar, you might incorporate various "solve the problem" activities, then encourage students to revisit their own works-in-progress, scanning vigilantly to identify and correct grammatical miscues covered in the lesson. Provide immediate and regular feedback during both drill and practice sessions and when new skills are being applied. Reduce the frequency of feedback proportionately as learning is mastered.

*For full citations, see "References" in Appendix.

Real-life Application:
Parents as Writing Partners
(prose/poetry)

When I began my teaching career, I asked myself the question, how do I get parents involved? I thought about my own children's education: How did I get involved with their schooling beyond the perfunctory level required by homework? I fondly recalled connecting with each of them through the very personal experience of reading together. Once my young sons became teenagers, however, I could not expect them to welcome me as a reading partner. I knew my boys would not hear of it, nor,

I suspected, would too many other teens. But how about writing partners? Would teens find it acceptable to become supportive writing partners with their parents? I knew that parents like me would get involved on a deeper level in their kids' learning if they had the right opening. I decided to try.

What evolved from this long-ago experiment is a weeklong program I now call "*Parents as Writing Partners.*" Semester after semester, it is this portion of my writing class that gets the most accolades from parents and students alike. *Parents as Writing Partners* truly marks one of the most rewarding experiences of my career. As students work with their moms, dads, and guardians as at-home writing partners, the writing skills they've learned in class are appreciably reinforced. And in the process, something wonderful happens: Students and parents get closer through the wonder of words. *Parents as Writing Partners* is a great way for teachers to fertilize positive memories at home while also grooming students to be lifelong lovers of learning. Over the years I have never tired of my additional students. And I cannot help but ask myself, how many of these wonderful stories

and poems would parents have written without the invitation to become their kid's writing partner?

So...Let the Writing Begin!

Once students have experienced their own writing process several times in the classroom, I send home the following invitation (Repro- graphic 6:5) and follow it up with a second invitation (Reproducible 6:6) the subsequent semester.

Dear Parents:

Won't you please join your son/daughter and me in an exciting opportunity to learn together? We would like to introduce you to our upcoming "Parents as Writing Partners" program. This weeklong home-based writing workshop gives your daughter/son the opportunity to guide you in an experiential writing process like the ones we've done in class. If you accept, you'll be lovingly guided through the following writing process by your son/daughter coach:

* Choose your own topic on which to write a short piece.
* Brainstorm ideas and feelings about your topic.
* Write a draft.
* Revise and edit draft to your liking.
* Produce a finished piece of prose or poetry.

Because <u>teaching</u> is one of the best ways to <u>learn</u>, I am sure you can appreciate the value this project will have on the growth of your daughter's/son's writing talents. While, of course, it is not mandatory, I hope you will accept this opportunity to write a piece for our workshop, and maybe even join us on "Author's Day"* next semester to celebrate ourselves as authors!

Thank you. I look forward to your response.

Sincerely,

*P.S. "Author's Day" provides the perfect setting to share the special work of parents (and their kids). It is truly a satisfying occasion to have family members sitting in our "author's circle," eating cookies together, and sharing their stories and poems.

Teacher Tip:
I always try to give parents plenty of notice when I send the invitation home, since many will have to adjust their work schedules to be present.

Dear Parents:

Do you remember how successful our first encounter with "Parents as Writing Partners" was? The class and I genuinely enjoyed reading each piece that was submitted, and you deserve another gigantic thank-you.

Now it's May and spring is in the air. Once again, your child is prepared to assist you and invites you to accept another invitation to experiment and celebrate as writers during "Author's Day" in our class. Here are the specifics:

Date:_____

Time:_____

Location:_____

Parking:_____

Thank-you for considering the project and remember, don't worry. You'll have your "coach" sitting next to you to offer assistance and encouragement along the way!

Sincerely,

Preparing Students to Be Writing Partners

Sometimes students adamantly contend their parents are too busy to get involved, but then are surprised to learn otherwise. With sufficient notice, many parents are willing to adjust their busy schedules to  accommodate an occasional school event. Many students tell me later they cannot believe how excited their parents were to participate. I love this!

Before I let learners loose on their parents, I remind them to use the same patience and encouragement at home that they offer their peers during conferencing sessions. I give them a set of guidelines (Reproducible 6:7) that we read and discuss together as a class. Then I ask them if they are ready to accept their role as writing teacher-facilitator-coach. Rarely do kids shy away from the challenge.

Writing Partner Guidelines

How to Help Your Home Partners:

1. Help your home partner choose a topic to write about (in the form of poetry or prose). It may be a memory that involves:

• A person

• An event

• A place

• A feeling

2. Help them brainstorm ideas and recall situations that stimulate strong images.

3. Help them write a draft. If necessary, record their prose or poem from dictation.

4. Define and explain line break and stanza if they choose to write poetry.

5. Help them revise and edit their work using the conferencing techniques and workshop strategies we use in class.

6. Help them write a final copy. Again, write or type from their dictation if necessary.

Invite your home partner to attend our future "Author's Day."

Dear _____:

Please accept my genuine appreciation for your cooperation during our "Parents as Writing Partners" project. The response was tremendous and I was impressed, once again, with the interest parents take in their children when they are invited to get involved.

If you were able to attend our Author's Day, I hope you enjoyed sharing and listening to the prose and poetry stimulated by this project.

Perhaps you will write more often now that you know you have a true writing partner eager and willing to share in the process! It's been a special year! Thank you for your contributions.

Sincerely,

Teacher Tip:
I always like send home a simple note of appreciation, such as this, to provide a sense of closure.

Parents as Writing Partners:
Celebrating Our Finished Products

Parents/guardians often write very poignant prose and poetry. Here are some examples from my own experiences with Parents as Writing Partners:

A Piece for My Daughters
I remember the day I learned I was going to have the both of you.
I was filled with so much emotion!
Fear, being a young first-time mother of twins!
Joy, the happiness I felt knowing you were both so perfect.
Excitement, having two angels.
Love, I already loved you so much!
Over the years of watching you grow, you continue to fill me with so much of the same emotion.
Fear, wondering if I might miss a part of helping you grow up.
Joy, watching you both blossom into beautiful young ladies.
Excitement, for what the future will bring into your lives.
And love, it is always there for you both, unconditionally, in my heart.
I love you both.

by Jodi (Aubree and Ashlee's mom)

October 1957
Fire!!! You can feel the heat
Fire!!! Do you ever give it a second thought?
I never did until October 1957
I stood on that corner for what seemed an eternity
Not reacting, not talking

Just watching this macabre dance of
flame destroy everything we owned.
We stood hugging and crying
The horrible feeling of having lost
our home
Mixed with our tears
The joyful feeling of being alive

by Jim (Danielle's father)

So Bright
This is for my sweet son Kevin
Who was surely sent from heaven
One gentle spirit, my delight
A boy whose star shines so bright!

by Nancy (Kevin's mom)

Matters of Life & Death
A warm summer's day
The smell of a rose
Playing cards at the kitchen table
There is no good-bye
You live on in my heart.

by Lisa (Jim's mother)

Closing and Opening
A
poem
can be a
musical way
home.

Teacher Tip:
When we invite parents to join us as writing partners, we not only expand students' appreciation and understanding of the writing process in a meaningful way, we nurture the very relationships that inspire authentic writing. Indeed, prose and poetry can be a musical way home.

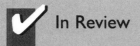 In Review

1. What is meant by authentic assessment?

2. Which brain-compatible principles support the use of rubrics as an important component of an authentic assessment system?

3. Do you presently use rubrics in your student evaluation system? If yes, how? If no, how might you incorporate them in the future?

4. Using the Instructor-Assessment Rubric (Reproducible 6:2), examine and assess the following three excerpts from an assignment that prompted learners to describe an autumn day.

Excerpts from "An Autumn Day"

Sample 1
One day I walked through the woods. I noticed the trees were very pretty. The colors of the leaves were beginning to turn. I like when that happens. They were gold and orange and red. The air was cool I could smell something burning.

Sample 2
The trees' look nice they are pretty. I like to walk threw the leaves, sometimes its windy. Then my friends and me go roller-blading. Roller-blading is cool my friends think their better than me no way! I'm the best. The other day I jumped over a gigantic ramp.

Sample 3
I heard footsteps crunch in the fallen leaves. A squirrel ran out to greet me. The air was cool and crisp. The leaves were golden and moving in the autumn breeze. I love autumn! I love the chill that makes me button my sweater as I stroll through the forest.

*A*ppendix

Writing Instruction Goals and Projects:
An Overview

Goal

I. TO DESCRIBE - *Use words that appeal to the senses in order to reveal appearance or to convey an image, impression, or feeling.*

Projects

- Write a paragraph describing a real or imaginary person
- or place.
- Create an advertisement for an object.
- Write a feature article describing a place or object.
- Create a classified advertisement to sell an article.
- Write a poem appealing to one or more senses.
- Pen a friendly letter.
- Write a journal entry; keep a journal for one week/month.
- Write a personal response to a particular book or piece of literature.

Goal

II. TO NARRATE - *Tell an imaginative (fictional) story or give an account of real events.*

Projects

- Write a narrative of an actual experience.
- Create a short story.
- Describe an event or experience in a journal entry.
- Pen a fable, folktale, or myth.
- Write a skit or script.
- Write a feature article.
- Create an autobiographical sketch.
- Write a humorous newspaper column.

Goal

III. TO EXPLAIN (Expository writing) - *Make factual information clear and understandable.*

Projects

- Write captions or labels
- Write a set of directions (how to)
- Write a letter of invitation
- Write a letter to the editor of the school newspaper
- Write a business letter
- Do a research report
- Write a news article and headline
- Create a biographical sketch based on an interview
- Write a biographical report
- Write an essay
- Do a character study based on a work of literature
- Write a letter of application
- Create a resumé

Goal

IV. TO PERSUADE - *Change the opinion of or influence the action of a particular audience.*

Projects

- Write an advertisement or commercial
- Send in a contest entry
- Write a letter (editorial) in favor of or against an issue
- Do a book review or literary analysis
- Write an opinion piece
- Write a review of an event or performance
- Write a formal speech

This overview was adapted from one prepared by Edith Wagner for the William Floyd School District in New York. It appeared on the back cover of student writing folders in Ms. Wagner's comprehensive K-12 writing program.

Five Core Propositions:
The National Board for Professional
Teaching Standards*

1. **Teachers are committed to students and their learning.**

2. **Teachers know the subjects they teach and how to teach those subjects to their students.**

3. **Teachers are responsible for managing and monitoring student learning.**

4. **Teachers think systematically about their practice and learn from experience.**

5. **Teachers are members of learning communities.**

*Reprinted with Permission from the National Board for Professional Teaching Standards. All rights reserved For more information on how to become a National Board Certified Teacher, call 800-532-1813 or visit www.nbpts.org.

Student Poetry Samples
Generated from the "Memory Lane" Prompt

Divorce
He squeezed my hand for the last time
As he let go, he winked and smiled
Adoringly...
My daddy sure must've been a handsome boy!

We raced down a beach dune
Collapsed in the sand
Laughing...
Complete Bliss!

I played the role of daddy's little girl
His "princess," he declared
Resting on a small park bench...
 Beautiful!

The warm, teal shimmered off the Atlantic
Through Kool-aid green palm trees
Feeling...
 Perfection!

Was it a dream?
The sun lightly kissed us
Indecisive palm fronds swaying like whispers in the summer
breeze...
 "Happy Birthday!"

He hugged me like I would never see him again
I was eight
Sitting in dead silence...
 "Beth"?

Divorce continued...

My pleading green eyes danced with golden, sunny glitter
He looked down and away unable to face curious eyes
Reflecting...
His own mother's

I stared in admiration
Anxiously awaited what he had to say
Swinging my feet...
Still too little to reach the sandy ground.

My long, blonde hair whipped around
In a sudden gust of wind
Stinging my eyes...
An excuse to cry.

By Beth (age 12)

Big Wheel Days
I remember my Big Wheel
It was my General Lee from the Dukes of Hazard
I was a Tough Guy with my blue, red, and yellow
Big Wheel with its over-sized plastic wheels
I could ride on two wheels tilted to one side
And make all the appropriate, five-year-old,
Mouth-made car sound effects
I still feel the same feelings driving around in my Camaro
Usually though
Without the sound effects

By Billy (age 12)

Activity Sheet:
Making Grammar Meaningful

Even a topic like "grammar" can be made meaningful with a little creative effort. The following activity is just one example. Many more await your discovery. Ask learners for help.

Red *Hot* Chili GRAMMAR

What do <u>adjectives</u> and <u>common</u> and <u>proper</u> nouns have to do with music?

You'll see!

Do Now:

<u>Think about</u> at least two of your favorite singers or music groups:

Example:

Mrs. Hanson's are: **Gloria Estefan**
                            The Doors

Why are the names of these singers and groups called <u>proper nouns</u>?

Musical Nouns and Adjectives

Name_____

Reminders:
<u>Common nouns</u> are people, places and things.
<u>Proper nouns</u> are specific people, places, and things.
They get capitalized.
<u>Adjectives</u> describe nouns.

Task: Change the following proper nouns to common nouns and adjectives and <u>use them in a sentence.</u>

Examples:
<u>The Doors</u> - I can't go to the movies until I polish all *the doors.*
<u>Sugar Ray</u> - The *ray* of sunshine faded like grains of *sugar* falling from the sky.

Third Eye Blind_____

_____

Silver Chair _____

_____

Red Hot Chili Peppers_____

_____

Goo Goo Dolls_____

_____

The Wallflowers_____

_____

Matchbox 20 _____

_____

Tonic _____

_____

All Saints_____

_____

Kid Rock_____

_____

Garbage_____

_____

Radish _____

_____

Spice Girls_____

_____

The Doors_____

_____

Offspring_____

_____

Back Street Boys_____

_____

Rage Against the Machine_____

_____

Go ahead and substitute some of these bands with your own favorites if you wish.

The Learning Pyramid National Training Laboratories

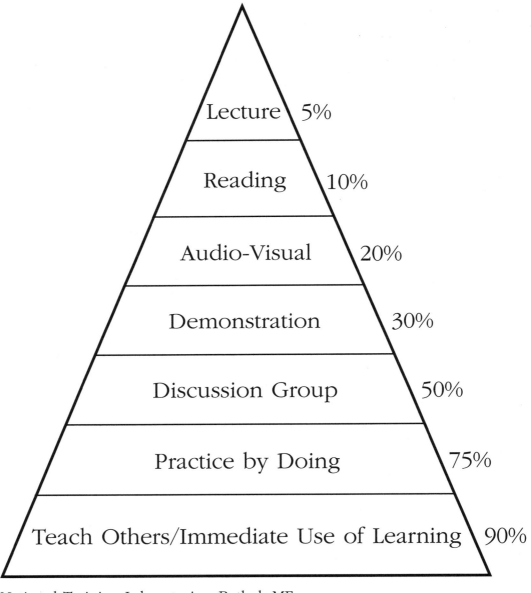

Lecture 5%

Reading 10%

Audio-Visual 20%

Demonstration 30%

Discussion Group 50%

Practice by Doing 75%

Teach Others/Immediate Use of Learning 90%

National Training Laboratories, Bethel, ME

WRITING RUBRIC & CRITERIA SCORE SHEET

Content

Content	6 Superior — Exceeds expectations	5 Strong — Shows control and skill, Many strengths evident	4 Maturing — Strengths outweigh weakness	3 Developing — Strengths and weakness are about equal, First draft effect	2 Emerging — Isolated moments of ability, Shortcomings dominate	1 Struggling — Results are lacking, Writer needs assistance
Ideas and Content Addressed	Exceptionally clear, Focused, Interesting	Clear, Focused, Interesting	Clear, Focused	Overly general, Predictable, Occasionally off topic	Somewhat unclear, Minimal development	Lacks central idea, Minimal development, Unclear ideas
Organization of Thoughts	Consistently strong, Effective sequencing	Strong, Effective sequencing	Sequencing clear, May be formulaic	Inconsistent, Undeveloped, Obvious	Lacking consistency//coherence	Lacking coherence, Disjointed
Word Choice	Exceptionally precise, Interesting	Precise, Interesting	Functional and appropriate	Ordinary, Lacking precision	Monotonous, Misused	Extremely limited, Vague, Imprecise
Sentence Fluency	Consistently strong, Varied, Expressive	Strong, Varied	Somewhat varied	Occasionally awkward	Awkward, Rambling	Incomplete, Awkward, Rambling, Obscured meaning
Voice (with respect to topic)	Exceptionally Expressive, Engaging	Expressive Engaging	Occasionally expressive, Engaging	Inappropriately personal or impersonal with audience	Mostly flat or overly personal or impersonal with audience	Flat, No sense of audience awareness
Conventions/Mechanics **Format** (relating to genre) **Paragraphing Mechanical Errors**	Very few errors, Barely noticeable	Few errors	Minor errors, Do not impede readability	Limited control, Errors begin to impede readability	Little control, Frequent and significant errors impede readability.	Numerous errors impede readability, Needs extensive editing.

Content Ideas and Content
• narrow topic
• fresh original ideas
• relevant quality details
• accurate supportive details

Organization
• inviting introduction
• thoughtful transitions
• sequencing—logical and effective
• pacing controlled
• flows smoothly
• satisfying conclusion

Style (The 3 style traits help produce personal writing style)
Style—Voice
• strong interaction between reader and writer
• appropriate for purpose and audience
• reflects strong commitment to topic

Style—Word Choice
• specific and accurate
• creates pictures
• effective verbs, nouns, etc.
• precise use of words

Style—Sentence Fluency
• well constructed sentences
• strong, varied, and purposeful sentence structure
• natural dialogue (if applicable)
• fragments, if used, add style

Conventions/Mechanics
• spelling, grammar, usage, paragraphing, capitalization

Student _____
Name _____

*This chart was developed using Arizona's Official Scoring Guide for AIMS, a six point.

READING RESPONSE RUBRIC & CRITERIA SCORE SHEET	4 Strong	3 Proficient	2 Maturing	1 Struggling
Response	Complex	Not as complex	Limited	Some attention to minor details of text
Understanding of Text	Thorough	Adequate	Limited	Little evidence of constructing meaning
Extension/Use of Text	Considerable, May be insightful	Minimal but appropriate	Inaccurate, Incomplete, Unfocused	Inaccurate, Incomplete, Irrelevant, Incoherent
Elements of Questions Addressed in Response	All	All	Few	No

Note1: How do you assess reading responses? Try this chart, developed from generic rubrics for reading formerly used in Arizona, which relies on benchmark indicators.

Note2: Some districts and states use a four- or five- point rubric system.

GROUP-WORK RUBRIC & CRITERIA SCORE SHEET

	6 Superior	5 Strong	4 Maturing	3 Developing	2 Emerging	1 Struggling
	Exceeds expectations	Shows control and skill, Many strengths evident	Strengths outweigh weakness	Strengths and weakness are about equal, First draft effect	Isolated moments of ability, Shortcomings dominate	Results are lacking, Writer needs assistance
Cooperation and Participation	Exceptional equity of sharing workload	Excellent equity of sharing workload	Evidence of sharing workload	Sharing work apparent most of the time	Inequitable unfair distribution of work	Unreasonable distribution of work. Requires intervention
Task Organization and Planning	Effective/logical sequencing of task objectives	Logical sequencing of task objectives	Sequencing of task objectives attempted	Sequencing of tasks attempted though gaps occur	Efforts seem random and without order	Random attempts to organize group, Requires intervention
Attention to Task	Exceptional and clear enthusiasm and effort	Clear enthusiasm and effort	Effort is evident	Sometimes distractions divert attention	Distractions divert attention	Numerous off-task distractions require intervention
Quiet Voices	Consistent clear evidence	Clear evidence	Evidence	Sometimes members distract others	Members often distract others	Inappropriate noise requires intervention
Completion of Task	Exceptional completion with insightful additions or variations	Fully completed with few editions	Completed	Basically completed	Lacks completion	Incomplete, Poorly done

Group Names/Overall Score

Name_____/_____Name_____/_____Name

Name_____/_____Name_____/_____Name

Note: Sometimes it is clear that one or two members of a group are not doing their fair share. Should you observe this common situation, you may wish to enter lower scores for these individuals. Class discussions on the challenges and fairness of group work and ensuring grades may encourage more individual responsibility within the group.

ORAL DEBATE RUBRIC & CRITERIA SCORE SHEET	6 Superior	5 Strong	4 Maturing	3 Developing	2 Emerging	1 Struggling
Attention to Appearance	Exceeds expectations	Shows control and skill, Many strengths evident	Strengths outweigh weakness	Strengths and weakness are about equal	Isolated moments of ability, Shortcomings dominate	Results are lacking
	Exceptionally well groomed	Excellent	Adequate	Some evidence of attention to appearance	Little evidence of attention to appearance	No evidence of attention to appearance
Logic of Argument	Exceptionally compelling, Clear sequencing	Effective sequencing	Clear, though may be obvious or simplistic	Inconsistent or confusing at times	Randomness or incoherence dominates	Lacking any logic or coherence of thought
Use of Statistics	Extremely effective, Strong correlation to argument	Effective selection	Good selection, Some data less useful than others	Adequate with some incorrect or irrelevant data	Irrelevant, Inaccurate selections	None and/or seriously incorrect or irrelevant
Citing Sources	Meets all requirements	Meets all requirements	Meets most requirements	Adequate with some minor errors	Errors compromise requirements	Little or no attempt at citation
Use of Charts and/or Graphs	Exceptional	Effective	Adequate	Some displays may be obvious or irrelevant	Mostly trite or irrelevant displays	Severely lacking, Irrelevant, or None
Opening Statement/Rebuttal	Compelling, Clear and focused	Fully developed with few editions	Clear and focused	Overly general or simplistic at times	Unclear, Minimal development	Lacks central idea

Team Names/Average Score:

Student Name _____ / _____ Student

Student Name _____ / _____

Name _____ /

Note: Sometimes it is clear that one or two members of a group are not doing their fair share. Should you observe this common situation, you may wish to enter lower scores for these individuals. Class discussions on the challenges and fairness of group work and ensuring grades may encourage more individual responsibility within the group.

ORAL PRESENTATION RUBRIC & CRITERIA SCORE SHEET

	6 Superior — Exceeds expectations	5 Strong — Shows control and skill, Many strengths evident	4 Maturing — Strengths outweigh weakness	3 Developing — Strengths and weakness are about equal, First draft effect	2 Emerging — Isolated moments of ability, Shortcomings dominate	1 Struggling — Results are lacking, Writer needs assistance
Presentation of Topic Addressed						
Eye Contact						
Poise with Attention to Audience/Other Group Members						
Vocal Expression, Enthusiasm						
Organization of Thoughts						
Accurate Examples, Details, Descriptions						
Response to Questions						
Preparation and Use of Visual Aids						

Try It Out! After examining the several completed rubric charts provided, work with colleagues to develop the criteria and benchmark language for the oral presentation chart above.

Recommended Resources

Brain-Compatible Instruction

A Celebration of Neurons by Robert Slywester

The Developing Mind: Toward a Neurobiology of Interpersonal Experience by Daniel Siegel, MD

Educational Leadership. Vol. 56, Number 3, November 1998. A comprehensive issue devoted to "How the Brain Learns"

The Emotional Brain: The Mysterious Underpinnings of Emotional Life by Joseph LeDoux

Emotional Intelligence: Why It Can Matter More Than IQ by Daniel Goldman

Magic Trees of the Mind: How to Nurture Your Child's Intelligence, Creativity, and Healthy Emotions from Birth to Adolescence by Marian Diamond and Janet Hopson. Dutton, 1998

Molecules of Emotion by Candace Pert

Teaching with the Brain in Mind by Eric Jensen

Why Zebras Don't Get Ulcers: A Guide to Stress, Stress Related Disease and Coping by Robert Sapolsky

Writing References

Coming to Know: Writing to Learn in the Intermediate Grades by Nancie Atwell

Differentiated Instruction by Carol Tomlinson

For the Good of the Earth and Sun: Teaching Poetry by Georgia Heard

In the Middle: New Understandings About Writing, Reading, and Learning by Nancie Atwell

Student-Centered Language Arts K-12 by James Moffett and Betty Jane Wagner,

Writing Without Teachers by Peter Elbow

References

Adams, Anne-Marie; Lorna Bourke; and Catherine Willis. Working memory and spoken language comprehension in young children. *International Journal of Psychology*. 34(5-6): 364-73.

Alcade, C.; J. Navarro; E. Marchena. 1998. Acquisition of basic concepts by children with intellectual disabilities using a computer-assisted learning approach. *Psychological Reports*. Jun; 82(3 Pt 1): 1051-6.

Aoki, H.; N. Yamada; Y. Ozeki; H. Yamane; N. Kato. 1998. Minimum light intensity required to suppress nocturnal melatonin concentration in human saliva. *Neuroscience Letters*. Aug 14; 252(2): 91-4.

Atwell, Nancie. 1998. *In the Middle: New Understandings about Writing, Reading, and Learning*. Boyton/Cook.

Audet, Richard; Paul Hickman; G. Dobrynina. 1996. Learning logs: A classroom practice for enhancing scientific sense making. *Journal of Research in Science Teaching*. 33(2): 205-22.

Bar-Tal, Yoram; Amiram Raviv; Ada Spitzer. 1999. The need and ability to achieve cognitive structuring: Individual differences that moderate the effect of stress on information processing. *Journal of Personality & Social Psychology*. July; 77(1): 35-51.

Boals A.; Klein K. 2001. Expressive writing can increase working memory capacity. *Journal of Experimental Psychology: General*; Sept. 130(3), 520-33.

Borella, Paola; A. Bargellini; S. Rovesti. 1999. Emotional stability, anxiety, and natural killer activity under examination stress. *Psychoneuroendocrinology*. Aug; 24(6): 613-27.

Bradley, Ann. 1998. A better way to pay; Feb. 25; *Education Week*. www.wcer.wic.edu/cpre/teachercomp.

Brandt, Ron. 1999. Educators need to know about the human brain; Nov; *Phi Delta Kappan*.

Britton, Bettis; Debra Virean. 1999. Effects of Supplemental Instruction on Undergraduate Academic Achievement, Motivational Orientations, and Learning Strategies. Dissertation Abstracts International; 59(10-A): April; p. 3831.

Cahill, Larry. "Emotions and Memory." Presentation at the Learning Brain Expo® Conference, San Diego, CA. January 19, 2000.

Campbell, Scott; Drew Dawson. 1990. Enhancement of nighttime alertness and performance with bright ambient light. *Physiology & Behavior*. Aug; 48(2): 317-20.

Carter, Cameron; Todd Braver; Deanna Barch, et al. 1998. Anterior cingulate cortex, error detection, and the online monitoring of performance. *Science*. 280: 747-9.

Chan, David; Neal Schmitt; Joshua Sacco; and Richard DeShon. 1998. Understanding pre-test and post-test reactions to cognitive ability and personality tests. *Journal of Applied Psychology*. June; 83(3): 471-85

Clement, Yan; Georges Chapouthier. 1998. Biological basis of anxiety. *Neuroscience & Biobehavioral Reviews*. 22(5): 623-33.

Cohen, Sheldon. 1999. Psychological stress and susceptibility to the common cold. *New England Journal of Medicine*. 32(9): 606-12.

Crowley, Kevin; Robert Siegler. 1999. Explanation and generalization in young children's strategy learning. *Child Development*; Mar-Apr; 70(2): 304-16.

Diamond, Marian. "What Do We Know from Brain Research?" *Educational Leadership*. Vol. 56, #3, November 1998. p. 11.

Elkind, David. 1999. Authority of the brain. *Journal of Developmental & Behavioral Pediatrics*. 20(6): 432-3.

Fan, Elliott; D. Gruenfeld. 1998. When needs outweigh desires: The effects of resource nterdependence and reward interdependence on group problem solving. *Basic & Applied Social Psychology*. Mar; 20(1): 45-56.

Filipczak, Bob (ed.). 1993. Why no one likes your incentive program. Aug; *Training Magazine*.

Frank, D. A., and M. E. Greenberg. 1994. CREB: A mediator of long-term memory from mollusks to mammals. *Cell*; 79: 5-8.

Frydenberg, Erica; Ramon Lewis. 1999. Things don't get better just because you're getting older: A case for facilitating reflection. British Journal of Education Psychology; Mar; 69(1): 81-94.

Gebers, Jane. 1985. Jigsaw puzzles: Rest for the left side of the brain. *Academic Therapy*. May; 20(5): 548-9.

Goodwin, J.E.; C.R. Grimes; J.M. Erickson. 1998. *Perception and Motor Skills*. Aug; 87(1): 147-51.

Grabe, Mark. 1992. Learning in technologically enriched study environments: Will students study effectively? *Reading & Writing Quarterly: Overcoming Learning Difficulties*. Oct-Dec 8(4): 321-36.

Hardy, L.; G. Parfitt. 1991. A catastrophe model of anxiety and performance. *British Journal of Psychology*. May; 82(Pt. 2): 163-78.

Hasselmo, M.E. 1999. Neuromodulation: Acetylcholine and Memory Consolidation. *Trends in Cognitive Science*; Sept; 3(9): 351-9.

Hudelson, Judith. 1997. Metacognition and journaling in process reading: Their relationship to reading comprehension and motivation to read. Dissertation Abstracts International, Section A: Humanities and Social Sciences. Sep; 58(3-A).

Jones, M. Gail, et al. 1999. The impact of high-stakes testing on teachers and students in North Carolina. Nov; *Phi Delta Kappan*.

Karni, A.; D. Tanne; and B. S. Rubenstein. 1994. Dependence on REM sleep of overnight improvement of a perceptual skill. *Science*; 265: 679-82.

Kellogg, J.S.; D.R. Hopko; M.H. Ashcraft. 1999. *Journal of Anxiety Disorders*. Nov-Dec; 13(6): 591-600.

Kudo, K. 1994. Locus of the retention benefits of variable practice in motor learning. *Shinrigaku Kenkyu*. Jun; 65(2): 103-11.

Laing, Sandra Peterson. 2000. The influence of language and cognitive abilities on comprehension in third-grade good and poor readers. Dissertation Abstracts International. (Humanities and Social Sciences); 60(8-A).

MacDonald, Angus; Jonathan Cohen; V. Andrew Stenger; Cameron Carter. 2000. Dissociating the role of the dorsolateral prefrontal and anterior cingulate cortex in cognitive control. *Science*. 288: 1835-8.

Malouff, John; N. Schutte. 1998. *Games to Enhance Social and Emotional Skills: Sixty-six Games that Teach Children, Adolescents and Adults Skills Crucial to Success in Life*. Springfield, IL, Charles C. Thomas Publishing.

Michael, Erika; Timothy Keller; Patricia Carpenter; and Marcel Adam Just. 2001. fMRI investigation of sentence comprehension by eye and by ear: Modality fingerprints on cognitive processes. *Human Brain Mapping*. 13(4): 239-52.

Miller, Ann; William Obermeyer; Mary Behan; Ruth Benca. 1998. The superior colliculus-pretectum mediates the direct effects of light on sleep. *Proceedings of the National Academy of Sciences*. July; 95: 8957-62.

Miller, Jan; Ann Goodyear-Orwat; Richard Malott. 1996. The effects of intensive, extensive, structured study on GRE scores. *Journal of Behavioral Education*. Dec; 64(4).

Nielsen, Bonnie Ann. 1999. The red studio: An exploration of the perceptual/cognitive workings of the 'enactive' mind. Contextual essay. Dissertation Abstracts International, Section A: Humanities and Social Sciences. Aug; 60(2-A).

Patton, J.G.; S.J. Woods; T. Agarenzo. 1997. Enhancing the clinical practicum experience through journal writing. *Journal of Nursing Education*. 36(5): 238-40.

Pennebaker J.W.; J.D. Seagal. 1999. Forming a story: The health benefits of narrative. *Journal of Clinical Psychology*. Oct. 55(10): 1243-54.

Ramirez, Al. 1999. Assessment-driven reform-The emperor still has no clothes. Nov; *Phi Delta Kappan*.

Rogers, D.A. 1998. Computer-assisted learning versus a lecture and feedback seminar for teaching a basic surgical technical skill. *American Journal of Surgery*; June: 175(6): 508-10.

Schmidt, R.A. and G. Wulf. 1997. Continuous concurrent feedback degrades skill learning implications for training and simulation. *Human Factors*; Dec: 39(4): 509-25.

Sephton, Sandra. 1996. The definition and measurement of chronic stress, and the effects of chronic stress on the cytotoxic activity of natural killer cells. Dissertation Abstracts International. May; 56(11-B): 6450.

Shafir, Uri; Morris Eagle. 1995. Response to failure, strategic flexibility, and learning. *International Journal of Behavioral Development*; Dec; 18(4): 677-700.

Sheline, Y.I.; M. Sanghi; M. Mintum. 1999. Depression duration but not age predicts hippocampus volume loss in medically healthy women. *Journal of Neuroscience*. Jun 15; 19(12): 5034-43.

Sirotnik, Kenneth; Kathy Kimball. 1999. Standards for standards-based accountability systems. Nov; *Phi Delta Kappan*.

Smith, Frank. 1995. Let's call education a disaster and get on with our lives; Apr; *Phi Delta Kappan*.

Smyth, J.; J. Souto; N. True. 2001. Effects of writing about traumatic experiences: The necessity for narrative structuring. *Journal of Social and clinical Psychology*. Summer: 20(2), 161-72.

Soffie, Monique; Kristin Hahn, Eriko Terao; F. Eclancher. 1999. Behavioral and glial changes in old rats following environmental enrichment. *Behavioral Brain Research*. May; 101(1): 37-49.

Stone, Mark. 1998. Journaling with clients. *Journal of Individual Psychology*. 54(4): 535-45.

Stone, Sandra; James Christie. 1996. Collaborative literacy learning during sociodramatic play in a multi-age (K-2) primary classroom. *Journal of Research in Childhood Education*. Spring-Summer; 10(2): 123-33.

Stuphorn, Veit; Tracy Taylor; Jeffrey Schall. 2000. Performance monitoring by the supplementary eye field. *Nature*. 408(6814): 857-60.

Sylwester, Robert. 1995. *Celebration of Neurons*. Alexandria, Virginia: ASCD.

Trinder, J.; S.M. Armstrong; C. O'Brien; D. Luke; M. Martin. 1996. Inhibition of melatonin secretion onset by low levels of illumination. *Sleep Research*. June; 5(2): 77-82.

van Praag, Henrietta; Gerd Kempermann; Fred Gage. 1999. Running increases cell proliferation and neurogenesis in the adult mouse dentate gyrus. *Nature Neuroscience*. 2(3): 266-70.

Wenzler, Ivo; Don Chartier. 1999. Why do we bother with games and simulations: An organizational learning perspective. *Simulation & Gaming*. Sept; 30(3): 375-84.

Willis, Scott (ed.). 1999. The accountability question; Nov; 41(7) *Education Update*: Association for Supervision and Curriculum Development.

Woodcock, Elizabeth; Rick Richardson. 2000. Effects of environmental enrichment on rate of contextual processing and discriminative ability in adult rats. *Neurobiology of Learning and Memory*. 73(1): 1-10.

About the Author

Anne Hanson, MA is a National Board Certified language arts teacher and a recognized staff developer with more than 15 years of classroom experience. She serves as a faculty associate at Arizona State University and is a published novelist. She is also the author of *Visual Writing*—a book of writing strategies for students, published by Learning Express. *Write Brain Write* is her first publication with The Brain Store™.

Index

Notes: